"Rappaport offers a range of spirit-lifting techniques for all . . . personality types."
—*The Cleveland Plain Dealer*

"[*The Family Gathering Survival Plan*] recogni[zes] that holidays are important, significant events in our lives, and that they bear an important relationship to not only the past but the present and the future."
—*St. Petersburg Times*

"For those whose holidays are stuck in a pattern of frustration and depression, Rappaport offers advice on how to beat the blues."
—*The Tennessean*

THE
FAMILY GATHERING
SURVIVAL PLAN

HOW TO MAKE

ALL YOUR FAMILY GATHERINGS

STRESS-FREE

Includes the 10 Commandments
for Celebrating Successfully

BY HERBERT RAPPAPORT, PH.D.

RUNNING PRESS
PHILADELPHIA • LONDON

9   8   7   6   5   4   3   2   1
Digit on the right indicates the number of this printing

Library of Congress Control Number 2002096252

ISBN 0-7624-1644-0
Cover designed by Whitney Cookman
Interior designed by Jan Greenberg
Edited by Danielle McCole
Typography: Stone Serif, Stone Sans, Perpetua

Previously published as *Holiday Blues*

This book may be ordered by mail from the publisher.
Please include $2.50 for postage and handling.
But try your bookstore first!

Running Press Book Publishers
125 South Twenty-second Street
Philadelphia, Pennsylvania 19103-4399

Visit us on the web!
www.runningpress.com

To my parents,

who taught me that

important traditions could be both

maintained and sculpted.

Contents

Acknowledgments

The Family Gathering Survival Plan is a different undertaking than other books that I have written. There were few established psychological theories to provide the conceptual framework for tackling a subject that is so universally experienced. Despite the impact holiday suffering has on so many individuals, little has been written on the subject. Thus, most of the labels that I developed to portray blues patterns needed to be conceived for the first time.

I am grateful to Dr. Suzanne Miller for her help in formulating a scheme for organizing patterns of holiday problems, and for contributing to the invention of a list of names. Our early discussions and shared perception of the problem provided an invaluable sense of motivation to undertake the project.

I would also like to thank Dr. Victoria Green for her professional hand in shaping the tone of the manuscript. Her timely input was invaluable in evaluating the applicability of these new groupings and their associated remedies.

I am extremely indebted to the creative staff of Running Press for their assistance and enthusiasm. Brian Perrin was instrumental in translating a raw idea into a book designed to address a broad cultural problem. I am thankful to Patty Smith, a very busy editor, who helped shape the manuscript while contributing solid ideas. I would also like to thank my typist, Eleanore Pulice, who turned out to be coach and mentor as she nurtured the manuscript in the most efficient way.

I would like to acknowledge all the clients whose lives have provided the material on which this book is based. Though I have worked hard to conceal their identities, I hope that as they find elements of their holiday dynamics, they are able to feel my gratitude for having had the opportunity to know and help them.

So much of what I know and understand about holidays is derived from my own experience. Holidays cannot be celebrated without the significant people who make up our lives. I would like to thank the friends who have participated in my holidays and the friends who have opened their celebrations to my family and me. I cannot fail to include my longstanding tennis group—Chip Butler, George Connelly, Tom Culp, Bert Keller, and Bill Miller—whose weekly ribbing was a reliable source of encouragement.

Finally, I am indebted to my family for providing the framework for appreciating and understanding celebration. As families evolve and change, so does the nature of how we spend our holidays. However, what remains constant is the way the blend of love, commitment, energy, and creativity has the power to turn occasions into precious times.

Introduction 1

For many years, the subject of holidays has been a central theme in my practice as a clinical psychologist. Interspersed throughout the year, they serve to highlight important universal, as well as personal, moments. Despite our tendency to consider them festive occasions for celebration, holidays seem to also cause a variety of problematic reactions.

As summer draws to a close, it is not too long before people in general, as well as those in my practice, begin the arduous task of getting ready for the high density of celebrations embedded in the fall and winter. Additionally, my occassional radio and television appearances always elicit a flurry of interest and search for more information. People, as always, take solace when they hear that their holiday blues are shared by others, and that discernible patterns can be consistently identified. Hearing such terms as Fixer, Perfectionist, or Poor Soul, they seem to take comfort in being able to apply a label to a reaction with which they have been struggling. Thus, my impetus for writing about holiday malaise comes from all those individuals whose celebrations are not always festive.

Each year, there is a resounding consensus that there is something missing from the way that we deal with holidays as a society. This ache for a more substantive experience is certainly most poignant during the winter holidays and the change of the calendar. However, other occasions, such as Mother's Day, Valentine's Day, birthdays, and anniversaries, as well as the multitude of religious and ethnic occasions, all have the potential to evoke powerful emotions. To be sure, sometimes holidays do represent what we expect—joyous celebrations that punctuate the passage of time. But there seems to be a growing tendency for people to actually dread these events. In fact, I have been able to organize these problematic reactions in terms of three dominant emotional responses: anxiety, depression, and anger.

As a psychologist, I have found that people are generally reluctant to face their problems head on. Often, they must be encouraged, cajoled, or pushed to become introspective and confront the concern as well as the possible solution. However, to acknowledge that problems exist certainly does not heighten or create the problem itself. As a profession, we in psychology are strongly committed to the notion that it is rarely better to "let sleeping dogs lie." Left unattended, self-defeating habits and approaches to life deplete our energy and, ultimately, have a demoralizing effect. This notion is reinforced around the year-end holidays when new and old clients alike admit that they need help, and that they will not spend one more holiday entrenched in a disheartening and painful syndrome. In other words, when it simply hurts too much, people will seek the help they need.

After working on holiday problems directly, or as a co-incidental part of the psychotherapy process, a number of clear ideas have emerged to help me confront some of the vexations that occur around the special times of life. After acknowledging and understanding the problem, some guidelines can be used to implement change. Hopefully, these ideas will benefit both the individual inclined to "self-help" as well as the practitioner who may be tackling holidays blues in the context of a professional relationship.

When we're children, holidays are times to anticipate and to enjoy. Spaced throughout the year, they suggest special meals, gifts, family gatherings, religious celebrations, and, perhaps most of all, vacation. Children, and to less of a degree, adults, look forward to breaks from school and work with an essential sense of enthusiasm. Resorts, restaurants, and even our transportation networks operate in synchronization with holiday—as anyone who has ever been at an airport around Thanksgiving can attest. Even our fuel prices fluctuate with the crush of driving associated with such holidays such as the Fourth of July and Labor Day. In many parts of the world, certain times of the year are clearly different because "the holidays are coming." No one would seriously try to conduct business in southern Europe as families slow down in anticipation of the traditional four-week August vacation. By the same token, one hesitates to get serious about things in the United States in the weeks before Christmas and New Year's, and would hardly expect to be successful pursuing job interviews as the year winds to a close in December.

Perhaps more than anything, holidays are calendar marks which suggest the gathering of families. In all parts of the world, individuals assemble with their relations and enact the drama of a particular celebration. In a single meal, a family's strengths, foibles, and skeletons can all be revealed. Going home is more than just a trip to a geographical location, especially given our increased mobility. Rather, it is a process through which we strengthen ties and allow ourselves to be immersed in memories, expectations, and relationships. Whether the experience is positive or painful, the family holiday helps define who we are.

Holidays, however, are much more than vacations from the tedium of everyday life. For children—who are free of the burdens of creating the magic associated with special occasions—holidays are the vehicle through which their hopes, fantasies, and beliefs are nourished. A child from a large family is the center of attention at her birthday party. A poor child manages to generate expectations of gifts or experiences outside the fold of normal life as Hanukah celebrations begin. The child from a dysfunctional family becomes hopeful that a celebration might transform the family into a harmonious group. When such transformation actually occurs, its effects can be far-reaching, and powerfully healing for both children and adults. More often, however, a child's hopes are not realized, so he or she must use the defensive fantasies especially available to children, in an attempt to weather powerful disappointment. Fortunately, children are resilient, and somehow recover enough to conjure another set of expectations for the following year.

In addition to the warmth and fun associated with special days, consider that the word *holiday* is derived from *holy day*. While not always evident, the majority of our "big" holidays are rooted in religion. There is widespread worry that the message of these holidays is lost by virtue of misplaced emphases, and that materialism has supplanted their significance as religious or spiritual celebrations. It is difficult to consider the subject of holiday blues without making reference to Christmas, even though many people in this culture and throughout the world do not celebrate it. Every year, the Christmas season seems to begin earlier. It is not uncommon to see the massive cultural transformation begin well before Thanksgiving, which used to be the kick-off point for the frenzy that continues to the end of the year. Mail-order catalogs begin to inundate us, stores are transformed by decorations, and television specials begin to proliferate as we prepare for this very expensive and time-consuming holiday.

Productions of such magnitude not only produce conflicts for the individual, but differences frequently develop within families, between generations and, mostly, between spouses. How many presents should the children get? How much money should we spend, and on whom? How do we alternate between at least two families of origin? (There can be even more, as we enter the terrain of reconstituted families involving children and spouses from prior marriages.) The collision between the secular conception of a holiday and the religious observance rears its head in exactly the same way. Our desire to get back to basics intensifies, perhaps after an effective guilt-inducing sermon delivered to a congregation already in conflict. Clergy of all denominations inevitably become spokesmen for the conflicts inherent in most holidays grounded in religion.

It is not only Christmas or the Christian holidays that generate potential conflict. Synagogues are well-known repositories of grand guilt for many Jews who attend services primarily around the "high" holidays, but neglect to come to weekly services. Rabbis over the years have conveyed their conflict over whether it is better to make those who attend services "feel good" or to do the annual guilt induction. Since the problem seems perpetual, it is my guess that neither really succeeds in causing better attendance throughout the rest of the year. Similarly, ministers who are personal friends have expressed similar sentiments about the crowd that shows up for Easter or Christmas service. Like their counterparts in other religions, Christian clergy wonder how much shame to arouse when the flock is in front of them, and whether they need to point out one more time that rabbits, baskets of goodies, and the coloring of eggs have nothing to do with the significance of Easter.

Holidays have an inseparable relationship with the passage of time. In one of my other books, *Marking Time*, I explored the various ways people have trouble with the organization and passage of time. Through the use of a tool I call "The Timeline", I spoke of how people tend to use special occasions as personal markers. These may be milestones such as graduations, births, deaths, and even highly personal events like a first kiss. Interspersed with these other events are holidays that have taken on special meaning, and therefore serve as positive or negative markers. It is not unusual, when probing an individual's earliest memories, to find that a particular holiday experience can stand out in a period of relatively little memory. Taken as a whole, these milestones provide a blueprint for how individuals evaluate their lives over time—past, present, and future. Using this time line approach in a series of studies I conducted over the past ten years, it has been possible to demonstrate that people have different temporal orientations which, in turn, affect their outlook, vitality and mood. These time orientations actually operate as enduring aspects of our personalities, according to recent research findings.

People oriented toward the past, for example, are vulnerable to feelings of anxiety and depression. They may grieve about their personal histories, neither living in the present nor having an outlook on the future. The result is that these individuals are characteristically sad, and may be prone to clinical depression under certain circumstances. People who are excessively future-oriented also fail to live in the present. They frequently "crowd" their futures with too many plans and goals, conducting their lives at a hectic pace as they attempt to implement the time line they envision. Though we generally think of living in the present as a positive thing, those who are too present-oriented tend toward exaggerated tendencies. We've all known people who "live for the moment." They usually have a difficult time with both tradition and planning, because neither the past nor the future seems to play an important role in their functioning.

When we consider "centered" individuals, we are really talking about people who are temporally balanced, in that they know where they've been, where they are and where they're going. Eric Erickson, the renowned psychoanalytic theoretician, referred to this kind of balance in terms of having an "ego identity." When an individual's identity is personally achieved, a sense of balance is solid and cannot be easily disturbed. On the other hand, when there is a weak sense of identity, or when it has been handed to an individual by parents, the balance becomes more precarious. Certain life events such as job losses, deaths in the family, or even career promotions can shift one's identity, thus creating an unbalanced time line resulting in psychological problems.

Holidays are important life events, as they simultaneously reflect and shape our identities. The awareness of an impending holiday evokes images and expectations in the immediate sense, while also prompting recollections, good and bad, of holidays past. Because of their capacity to produce conflict and tension in our life lines, they can challenge our sense of identity. Things may be going along just fine when all of a sudden a significant religious holiday occurs. Questions about observance begin to occupy our mental life, along with all the possible questions commonly associated with planning celebrations. While we might think that such issues wane with age, in fact, holiday induced tensions tend to persist throughout life, especially for those of us whose values and identities remain in a perennial state of flux.

Karen, an acquaintance in her mid-fifties, recently announced to her family that she wanted to recapture the simplicity of childhood Christmas celebrations. She invoked the "only handmade presents" rule, which seems to be a frequent universal hedge against the commercialism of the holiday. As is often the case, her attempt to get more comfortable with her values produced protests from her three young children, who had definitely developed a taste for action figures and video games which clearly could not be produced by hand. Rather than suggesting resolution through family discussion, or even by accepting his wife's proclamation, Karen's husband under-mined her, as he had done in prior situations, by taking the children's side. A fight of enormous proportions ensued, which ended in Karen actually leaving for the holiday. We began family therapy after the New Year, with fortunate and favorable results.

While this situation might seem extreme, holidays ac-tually do evoke very strong reactions in different individuals for different reasons. Karen was dissatisfied with several as-pects of her lifestyle, and with the way she perceived her chil-dren to be developing. Recalling prior Christmas holidays, and how they never seemed to reflect her desires or remembrances from her own childhood, she took provocative action. Ultimately, it was not effective.

The way Karen found herself celebrating Christmas as an adult presented a challenge to her identity. She wanted to make the holiday more consistent with her past, a truer re-flection of her values. The problem is that holidays are not cel-ebrated in a social vacuum. One cannot make changes, even when they seem right, in a unilateral way. Instead, a process involving discussion and mutual understanding must occur.

Holidays, in short, are calls to action, fueled by a complex set of emotions ranging from anxiety to sadness to anger to paralysis. While my view of this subject is colored through my clinical lenses, I am talking about many indi-viduals and many holidays. It is fascinating to observe how intense people become around the middle of October, for Thanksgiving, Christmas, and New Year's Eve all involve planning, which many find overwhelming. A 42-year-old male client, who was trying to deal with two sets of children from two marriages, plus an angry ex-wife and demanding new in-laws, exclaimed, "I wish I could go to sleep on November first and not wake up until January second." For those who think that such a jaded reaction toward celebrations represents a minority of neurotic patients, it is reassuring to note that it is usually specific holidays which are distressing for different individuals. In other words, someone can enjoy and look forward to most celebrations, but have pause when it comes to a certain day.

Dick, for example really loved the fall and winter holidays, but absolutely fell apart when it came to New Year's Eve. His situation provides a very good example of how holidays interact with time, as I discussed above. Dick loved to throw himself into the fall holidays, savoring their immediacy without much thought of the past or the future. As the new year approached, however, it was a different story. Like many of us, he would cautiously begin to formulate those infamous plans for the coming year that we call "resolutions." Each year, he made the same mistake, by setting too many unrealistic goals that had not been realized in previous years. Predictably, the result of this painstaking ritual was self-denigration—almost before he had a chance to test the validity of the current year's resolutions. This pattern of self-defeating goal setting caused profound disappointment, sadness, and, in Dick's case, a significant depression that lasted until the end of February.

The basic plan of this book is to catalogue the variety of ways that people respond to significant holidays in their lives. Years of professional practice have shown that most commonly, anxiety, depression, and frustration/anger are the problematic emotional responses to special occasions. Within each of these emotional groups, there are discernible sub-categories. A familiar example is the Perfectionist, whose predominant response to certain holidays will be anxiety. The Juggler will also respond with anxiety and apprehension, but for a different set of reasons. For the Mourner, holidays mean a melancholy revisitation of times past, while the Fixer considers them an exercise in futility, and feels frustrated as he attempts to change the behavior of others.

The Holidays: 2
An Overview of Our Celebrations

When we think of the holiday blues, inevitably our minds turn to the protracted period, governed by Thanksgiving's approach, that signals the countdown to Christmas, Hanukah, and the new year. Most treatment of holiday malaise in television, radio, and the print media focuses on this period, with experts dispensing advice about how to avoid the pitfalls of overspending, overextending, and maintaining the holiday spirit. Occasionally, these approaches even address post-holiday blues, but they are usually concerned only with the period following the winter celebrations.

It has been my experience, however, that people react to a much wider variety of special occasions that occur throughout the calendar year. Thus, while some individuals are perfectly fine with Christmas, they may have a very strong negative reaction to a seemingly neutral holiday such as July Fourth, or a very sad response to a strictly personal milestone such as an anniversary or birthday—even during the prime of life.

Different personality types and problem patterns tend to be exacerbated by different times and rituals, and the expectations associated with them. Let's look more closely at the special occasions that trigger blues patterns involving anxiety, depression, and anger. For purposes of organization, I have divided the holidays into three distinct types: religious holidays, universal secular holidays, and personal holidays.

Religious Holidays

These occasions may have originated through observance, but they've evolved into powerful annual rites with strong personal, social, and economic significance. Because we are a heterogenous society, there are many holidays associated with different ethnic and religious groups too numerous to acknowledge here. The exclusion of African-American, Asian, Native American, Islamic, Russian Orthodox, and other celebrations, is by no means intended to diminish their meaning. Based on preliminary discussions with individuals whose holidays were not included, they seemed to be able to find themselves within the "blues profiles" outlined in the next chapter.

◆ *Christmas and Hanukah* ◆

Though they occur during the same month, these holidays obviously do not have the same religious significance. In some sense, they are in direct competition. Christmas is not just a day, for it represents an ever-expanding season that seems to kick off soon after the beginning of the school year in September and continue to the end of the calendar year.

The impact is even greater in lower schools, where rehearsals begin for holiday plays and pageants, carols are sung, and the countdown for winter recess is eagerly anticipated. This period has become so significant that normal business is transformed, and in some cases suspended, until after the new year. Even decisions to fire employees are often deferred by employers who do not wish to be seen as inordinately cruel. Charitable drives are begun as an attempt to connect with the generous spirit of the season.

The centerpiece of the Christmas season is, without doubt, Santa Claus and all he connotes. Santa is what stirs the hope and imagination of children, and what sets off frenzy in the marketplace. The annual rite of shopping for gifts begins with a fury, taxing the budgets of most mortals while providing the nation's merchants with hope of ending the year in the black. The persona of Santa, a mythical figure, creates the secular color of the holiday and, in turn, the potential for the stresses and strains associated with Christmas. It is no wonder, then, that non-Christians who celebrate holidays during this time feel some desire to present an attractive counterpoint to the other compelling activities of the season. While some non-Christians see the holiday as primarily secular, and partake in the tree decoration along with the acceptance of a

non-religious Saint Nick, it is accurate to say that many simply do not.

Hanukah, the Jewish festival of lights, usually falls
earlier in December than Christmas. While it has been on
the Hebrew calendar since 65 B.C., its juxtaposition with
Christmas has prompted many Jewish families to go beyond
the simple lighting of the menorah, and step up the magnitude of gift-giving, which extends over the eight days of the
holiday. In cases of "ecumenical" families, or interfaith marriages, there is often an attempt to celebrate both holidays—
an obvious potential basis for the seasonal blues.

One of the most powerful things that happens in this
season is the assemblage of families. As Christmas Eve approaches, the entire country begins to shut down. Children,
already out of school, are joined by adults, except for the
skeletal crews who staff transportation, telecommunication,
emergency health care, and convenience food enterprises. It
is the sustained connection to both nuclear and extended
families that creates possibilities for the highs and lows associated with this holiday. Emotions run very high as familiar
patterns of interaction occur in the context of gift exchanges,
religious worship, or the eventual settling-in for a family
meal. It is this period, more than any other, which triggers
the holiday blues patterns.

◆ *Easter and Passover* ◆

As with Christmas and Hanukah, these holidays usually fall
close together, depending on the vagaries of the solar and
lunar calendars. Though obviously different in religious con-

tent, it is significant that both occur around the beginning of spring, when people's appetite may again be amenable to celebration after the dormancy of winter. These occasions may have greater religious significance than the winter holidays, but they really don't capture a big piece of the calendar. While the Jewish holiday of Passover technically lasts a week, most families limit the celebration to one or two Seder nights where special foods are eaten. Easter always occurs on the first Sunday following the full moon on or after March 21, the vernal equinox when hours of day and night are equal in length. Though arguably the most significant holiday for the Christian faith, it does not seem to have the evocative power of Christmas. The Easter Bunny, the egg hunt, the baskets of chocolate rabbits, jelly beans, and colored eggs have become secular aspects of Easter which do not involve exhausting amounts of preparation or creativity. As at Passover, there is a traditional family meal on Easter Sunday, but typically neither of these celebrations stirs the blues patterns as much as the more turbulent winter holidays.

Increasingly, both holidays are celebrated by local family members, as demonstrated by the lesser degree of travel as compared with Christmas or Thanksgiving. However, even the most benign holidays can arouse blues patterns *if they involve the assemblage of families.* Anyone who has attended a Seder will probably recall a fair amount of disagreement about such issues as the length of the meal or the degree to which the reader adheres to the letter of the Haggadah, or prayer book. A young client of mine recently related that a major family rift occurred during his Passover meal because several family members thought he was "showing off" when he attempted to display a newly discovered appreciation of the Hebrew language.

Similarly, a recently married Christian couple had a surprisingly intense battle over different expectations associated with the celebration of Easter. Both had children from prior marriages, and the children created some tensions by invoking memories of how the holiday had been celebrated within their original families. Insecurities and poor negotiating skills allowed what appeared to be solvable differences to escalate into a full-blown conflict, which luckily found itself quickly onto the agenda of their next marital psychotherapy session.

Universal Secular Holidays

These holidays are spread throughout the calendar year and vary in their level of significance. The only reason I mention some of them is that, over the years, I have found that many individuals mention a particular holiday which they either love or despise. In either case, there is always the potential for elevating expectations or completely avoiding certain holiday rituals. It is fascinating to step back and examine the days on the calendar which are denoted as holidays. Each country has its important days, which reflect both the historical and current values of that culture. I recently learned that Barcelona, Spain celebrates 140 religious festivals annually. In the United States, our secular holidays deal with love, the honoring of parents, special presidents, and fallen war heroes, in addition to the acknowledgment of significant days in the emergence of our republic. We also dedicate a day to the warding off of evil spirits, express our gratitude to native Americans for aiding in the survival of English settlers and, of course, must contend with the day that connotes that another year has ended.

One of the strengths of our culture is our willingness to accommodate novelty. Dr. Martin Luther King Jr. Day, Earth Day, and Secretaries' Day honor new heroes, in addition to focusing on themes which reflect the evolving values of our society. While it can always be said that some of these occasions are invented by greeting card companies, they nevertheless take on meaning to the individuals involved. Secretaries who are not acknowledged on this relatively new celebration are apt to feel hurt, especially if their peers receive recognition. In the pages that follow, a sample of some of these holidays will be provided in the hope that one or more have a special significance.

◆ *Valentine's Day* ◆

Legend has it that Saint Valentine wrote a tragic love letter to his sweetheart on the day of his death. Thus, each year on February 14, we traditionally acknowledge romantic interests or spouses with gifts of candy, flowers, intimate personal garments, or minimally, an expressive card. As with so many of our holidays, Valentine's Day has become enlarged and extended to include a wider radius of love connections, especially children. Needless to say, the greeting card and rose enterprises flourish along with manufacturers of confection. Established couples tend to seek romantic trysts, either at home, in restaurants, or with "get-away weekends."

Valentine's Day seems to be slanted toward women more than men. Starting in middle school, many girls become disaffected if they are not someone's Valentine, as expressed by a card, note, or covert communication through a common friend. This acknowledgment becomes more important as they reach puberty and begin to define one aspect of their self-esteem in terms of the interest expressed by boys. The feminist movement notwithstanding, females tend to expect attention on this day, and are the ones more prone to be hurt by negligent behavior. Most men I have known are a bit cynical about Valentine's Day, but usually do something rather than generate unnecessary conflict in their relationship. Most children are content to let the holiday slip by without great expectations, but do not mind finding a few hearts filled with candy. The potential for holiday blues seems to occur when this day is used as a barometer of the romantic quality of individuals' lives.

A woman with whom I recently worked saw the behavior of her husband around Valentine's Day as a trigger to seriously consider divorce. Despite the fact that she continuously alerted him to the importance of these sentimental opportunities, he frequently accused her of being "brainwashed by Hallmark," and would not allow himself to address her needs. She said that despite the seemingly trivial aspect of her hurt, it clarified just how many of her needs were acknowledged only as being "corny and sentimental." Fortunately, her husband was open to addressing her reaction and decided to work on their marriage in a constructive therapeutic process. Interestingly, he has continued psychotherapy on his own and seems to have made an about-face. Now, he claims to have been a "closet" romantic all along!

◆ *Summer Holidays* ◆

On first consideration, Memorial Day and Independence Day seem like innocuous, pleasant lead-ins to summer. For most of the country, this suggests warm weather and activities involving water, beaches, outdoor sports, and family picnics. It is fair to ask how such seemingly pleasant images can in any way be associated with holiday blues. But remember, the same question can be asked about Christmas—and it often is. For families, the greatest source of stress is the fact that Memorial Day means that school is out, or soon will be. This creates a strain for working parents, as their children's lives become much less structured. Even when camps are involved, time schedules change, there is no homework to occupy children before and after dinner, and bedtimes inevitably slide forward. Most parents hate to admit it, but there is often a quiet dread as summer recess begins, and a noticeable anticipation during the final days of August. At least it is safe to say that most working parents are in conflict between the freedom summer ought to mean, and the strain it puts on their schedules and budgets.

Many people become upset as summer holidays approach because they are not ready to remove their clothes and present themselves in swimwear on beaches and at poolside. You can tell when it's almost summer by the sharp increase in health club enrollments and the appearance of new diet plans in publications and on television. Lean and fit bodies appear on the covers of men's and women's magazines as a reminder that it is time to "shape up." The deadly combination of physical vanity plus the inability to live up to goals which can, as we all know, be quite unrealistic, may result in anxiety or depression.

The other major component of these holidays involves tradition and family gatherings. The assemblage of nuclear and extended families around the barbecue has become fairly typical throughout the United States. As such, all the potentially troublesome feelings, dynamics, and behavior patterns can erupt when there is pressure to construct a special party, or when the particular mix of relatives or friends is disturbing. For example, a health-minded young man, whom I have seen professionally, dreaded the teasing he inevitably received from his father because of his refusal to partake in the traditional steaks that were grilled for the family Fourth of July picnic. Each year, the predictable razzing would awaken memories of a long, unhappy adolescence in which he felt he never measured up to an unclear set of parental expectations.

◆ *Halloween* ◆

This is a unique and intriguing holiday in that it taps into two different dimensions of ourselves. We can choose to give or accept an invitation to a costume party, which might either be great fun or extremely anxiety-provoking. Some individuals simply rent any old costume or throw one together without much deliberation. Others see the masquerade as a serious expression of themselves, and may belabor the choices of who they will be. These days, there is the fear that our choice will expose something from our unconscious. It probably will, but so what? Should a meek man decide to dress as Julius Caesar, or dare to cloak himself in the ominous black robe of Darth Vader? Should a woman who secretly desires to be more glamorous choose a "shockingly" revealing version of Cleopatra?

In addition, there are all the possibilities for relating to the primitive aspects of the holiday. Halloween, after all, has its roots in the Celtic festival of Samhain Eve, during which huge bonfires were lit on hilltops to frighten away evil forces. Because souls of the dead were thought to return on that night, the holiday became associated with scary images of ghosts, witches, and demons. Since Halloween was secularized in the late nineteenth century, individuals have begun to choose costumes representing such horror figures as Count Dracula, Dr. Hannibal Lecter (*Silence of the Lambs*), or Darth Vader (*Star Wars*). Before the final decision can be made, the question of "how do I really see myself?" can become so strenuous that many people simply decline invitations to costume parties. Abstaining from masquerading is unfortunate, since Halloween may provide an opportunity for integrating some disparate elements of one's personality. In cultures where Mardi Gras is acknowledged, the celebration actually marks a season rather than representing a one-night transformation. In addition, tribal cultures, where masks are used, find great value in expressing inhibitions and conflict in the context of the masquerade.

Ironically, similar stress can occur for adults who need to dress their children for the trick or treat segment of Halloween. Some parents get caught in the perfectionist's need to produce the perfect costume. After all, its quality and creativity can be construed as a reflection on its inventor, so great efforts are not uncommon. Halloween has recently seen a dramatic rise in stature, so that in addition to carving one or more jack-o-lanterns, people have taken to decorating their homes with orange lights or other symbols of the holiday. If October 31 does not fall on a weekend, the strain on busy families can be evident as preparations are made without the benefit of days off from work or school. This pattern of holiday perfectionism will be revisited in some of the profiles in the next chapter. For now, it is important to address the basis for celebration: tradition, meaning, and most of all, fulfillment. Contemporary dual-career or single parents are often hard pressed to make an imaginative costume from scratch. It would be far better, with the child's input, to do something that contributes to the good humor of the day, rather than letting perfectionism defeat the basic light-hearted nature of Halloween.

◆ *Thanksgiving* ◆

This very popular, deeply American holiday has its roots in the invitation to celebrate the harvest, extended by the Pilgrims to Native Americans in 1621. Almost everyone claims that Thanksgiving is high on his or her list of favorite holidays. It cuts across religious, ethnic and political lines to form a family-oriented feast in the heart of autumn. There are no gifts to buy, and only the most basic religious overtone takes the form of expressing gratitude; as such, it can be adapted to just about any format. The emphasis is on the great meal that centers around a turkey and, for some families, also the mandatory watching of a football game on television. So, one might legitimately ask, what are the possible blues patterns for this holiday which is as straightforward as apple pie?

The first stress trigger is associated with the scope of meal preparation, which usually falls to the women of the household, despite purported advances in the division of household labor. Perfectionism and conflict associated with unfair distribution of labor are certainly areas of potential trouble. In many families, men can no longer lounge around the TV while women do the lion's share of food preparation and serving. Tensions that already might be high can really escalate in the mix of resentment and guilt that all too frequently erupts.

Another form of stress reaction occurs when complex family loyalties generate conflicts concerning where the celebration will occur, and who will be there. As families tend to grow geographically distant, young married couples or grown children of divorced parents have to carefully decide about rotations, and often experience stress when they are in "no-win" situations in which someone is bound to get his or her feelings hurt. Ironically, one of the greatest sources of potential stress has to do with one of the most desirable aspects of Thanksgiving: the opportunity for communication and the absence of special activities.

Dysfunction patterns seem to occur when families with intense unresolved issues are thrown together for more time than they are accustomed. Just such a scene erupted in the film *The War at Home* where anxieties and anger became magnified in a household with a troubled young man (Emilio Estevez) who is unable to shed the trauma he experienced in Vietnam. An explosive scene occurs between the young veteran and his father (Martin Sheen) whom he blames for going to Vietnam in the first place. The young man ends up leaving home after a potentially violent interaction, when one is not sure whether there will be a suicide or homicide. While most disturbing transactions certainly lack this level of drama, many of my patients have come back from what should have been wonderful family celebrations distraught by all-too-familiar patterns which have upset them for much of their lives.

A tangential but equally significant source of tension in this otherwise ideal day is that it represents the beginning of the hectic holidays, immediately on the horizon. For those upset by the Christmas/Hanukah season, Thanksgiving has increasingly been recognized as the launching point for some very serious blues patterns. In fact, the day after Thanksgiving is widely accepted as "Black Friday" since merchants universally expect to benefit from the first Christmas shopping spree, and hence find their books "in the black".

◆ New Year's Eve ◆

Despite the effort people put into letting the end of the calendar pass without great upheaval, most of us have our own ways of both celebrating and coping with this potentially powerful transitional day. Many try to mark the passage of time in some special way, ranging from the traditional New Year's Eve party to simple gatherings with friends or family. We all know people who actually exhibit irritation with all the fuss and elect to avoid the drinking, crowds, and dangerous driving situations along with all the pressure to "celebrate" by disengaging and going to bed without "seeing the ball drop."

However we choose to celebrate—or not to celebrate—this occasion, it does not go by without stirring deep emotions. Unlike other holidays, there is little or no activity related to meals, and in most cases, no attention to extraordinary purchases. Try as we may to discount the significance of the passage of time, New Year's Eve and the days that follow are times for self-evaluation and reflection. The new year illuminates the orientation people have to marking time. Past-oriented individuals may become morose, while reflecting on the unfinished business of the past or on their personal disappointments. Others who are very goal-directed and live in the future tend to overload themselves with both real and lofty resolutions. These self-promises may range from weight and health concerns to major changes in lifestyle, jobs, or even their personal value systems.

The process of making resolutions may be a constructive enterprise if goals are grounded in the identity of the individual, and are both realistic and sincere. Sometimes we dabble in changes only to see ourselves disappointed, and then we start to distrust the validity of our own intentions. I generally encourage people to treat the New Year holiday as a break from routine, or a chance to travel. The time to take inventory of one's life is always available and, if it is not distilled to a particular calendar day, might actually stand a chance in creating a serious life alteration. For many individuals, being nudged into contemplating the future is a disturbing experience. In fact, based on my research, producing a time line tied to anticipated milestones is an arduous task for even the hardiest of souls. We find an appreciable discomfort when subjects are asked to document the major events in their past, present and future.

As is common practice, I recently asked a woman in her thirties who was having career issues to create a time line so that we could have a dialogue about her changing jobs. I gave her the blank form I have used for this research, and she enthusiastically said she would return it the following week. After three weeks went by, I inquired about the status of the assignment. She went into her purse and pulled out the blank paper, sheepishly handing it to me while saying she couldn't, or maybe wouldn't, do it. Something comparable to this happens to many people around New Years Eve; they start to think about the future, get very anxious, and look for a way to rid themselves of the burden. It is not surprising mental health professionals get a lot of calls around this time of year. Individuals might be feeling depressed, angry, anxious, or some combination of these emotions as a reaction to the sequence of "heavy duty" holidays, or the plunge into a new calendar year may have simply put them over the edge.

Apart from the task of evaluating one's life and making commitments to change, there is the question of how to celebrate the occasion itself. The young and energetic have always wanted to congregate in open spaces, like Times Square in New York City. Lacking the fortitude to plunge into that sea of expectant individuals, many people at least watch the ball drop on television. The mood is one of desired and sometimes forced elation. Alcohol, ranging from beer for the young to champagne for the more mature, is meant to be plentiful, to ensure a party atmosphere. Needless to say, New Year's Eve is synonymous with excess indulgence. One of the holiday blues personality profiles which will be discussed later, the Merrymaker, is particularly prone to such excess, and may find support and encouragement on a holiday strongly associated with intoxication.

Intoxication, however, is no safeguard against the multitude of feelings that come up as we anticipate another year.

Our senses may become dulled, but we find that the difficult themes of our lives are still there. It is not uncommon to see guests at a New Year's Eve party lapse into a state of melancholy. Sometimes, the sense of gravity comes from a less than hopeful feeling about the short-term future. Sadness can also be triggered by memories of past celebrations that remind us of past relationships. The important point is that alcohol, intended to elevate the spirit, cannot protect us from the realities of our lives. The Merrymaker, in particular, usually discovers that there is a significant emotional price to pay when the party comes to its inevitable end.

Personal Holidays

Birthdays, anniversaries, graduations, and vacations are different in that they do not occur on a broad cultural basis. Instead, they happen for individuals, involving the friends and family to whom they are most connected. However, what we expect to feel and do on these special days is indeed influenced by our social context. Different families have their own ways of acknowledging occasions, as do different ethnic groups and social classes. Nevertheless, these personal occasions all have the potential to evoke the same blues patterns as the universal holidays.

◆ *Birthdays* ◆

The celebration of birthdays has its roots in childhood as most families, especially nowadays, make a big fuss over children's birthdays. Whereas in the past, small family gatherings were generally limited to the traditional cake and a few presents, the modern family tends to extend itself to a much larger arena at a surprisingly young age. These birthday extravaganzas often involve large segments of the children's nursery school or elementary school class, with 20 or more children in attendance. Depending on the families' economic status, the parties can occur in settings such as the local Y, fast food establishments, sports events, or movie theaters. Based on personal experience, I can say that, while these celebrations can be great fun (for the kids), managing to feed and entertain large numbers of children, most of whom are unknown to the host family, can be pretty intense. Perhaps the ultimate case of the birthday/religious rite of passage is the bar or bat mitzvah, marking the thirteenth year for observant Jewish children. In the most extreme cases, these events, often to the chagrin of the religious educators, can be extravagant catered affairs, as expensive and complex as weddings. They can upset families in a number of ways. Intergenerational conflict can arise over the perceived departure from the spiritual nature of the religious ceremony, or the economics of such large catered affairs can cause tremendous strain and value-based conflicts.

As these modern birthday celebrations may be stressful on several fronts, they are potential catalysts for the same blues patterns as holidays that trigger perfectionism and overextending tendencies. Generally, birthday celebrations start to shrink by late childhood, and continue to change. Except for the "big ones" (40, 50, 60, etc.), birthdays become smaller affairs, mostly shared by intimates; some individuals prefer that the day simply slips by. As we age, birthdays become, in a sense, a personal new year celebration, and the reactions can be comparable to those on New Year's Eve. Some yearn for the lost splendor or innocence of youth, while others feel bitter about the velocity of their aging process. A major factor in birthdays is marking the point they represent on our personal time lines.

A male client who had just turned 40 was deeply upset because he felt he should have been more established and been a homeowner, rather than a mere renter, at this ripe age. By exploring the origins of his self-imposed deadline, we were able to ease the pain as he came to understand the arbitrary quality of such a premise. Birthdays often evoke anxiety, depression, and/or anger in relation to issues such as marital and reproductive status. In the past decade, I have had to confront the dynamics of the biological clock with many female clients who deferred too long the decision to have a child, or simply were not fortunate in terms of relationships. Thus, beware when you offer someone a well-intended birthday wish, as it is not always possible to know the meaning of that personal marking point. Finally, since a birthday involves only one celebrant, it is easy to make an assessment of how we are valued depending on what others do for us. Cards, telephone calls, gifts, along with the staging of adult parties, all have the potential to either please or upend, depending on the recipient. A word of caution about surprise parties: know who the person is, and make sure that he/she will be grateful, not chagrined, at the surprise.

◆ *Anniversaries* ◆

While anniversaries may celebrate any occasion, we usually think of marriage. Unlike birthdays, which are entirely personal, wedding anniversaries acknowledge the growth of a relationship. Couples seem to develop their own special way of addressing their wedding anniversary, though it is somewhat expected that men extend themselves as a gesture of gratitude. This male gesture has been the object of much media attention as we often see the sitcom guy in trouble because he's forgotten the special day. Florists say that they thrive on the guilty male who almost let his anniversary slip by. This stereotype of the forgetful male is probably undergoing substantial revision as a reflection of changing gender roles. Nevertheless, a substantial amount of disappointment can surface when this important date is neglected. It is always important to acknowledge marriage or other relational anniversaries, even if one member of the couple resists. When it comes to the art of celebration, effort is surely required. The problem is that our fast-paced lives often provide an excuse for not extending ourselves. Since an anniversary gesture involves one person with whom we are intimately familiar, the note, card, or gift should take on a special significance. Of course, realistically, sometimes all is not well with a relationship, and the consideration of a gesture becomes mired in conflict. Sometimes individuals discover their feelings for their significant other when it comes time to express themselves on their anniversary.

There is another kind of anniversary which, as a psychologist, I feel compelled to mention. People often have very powerful emotional responses to calendar days that mark highly specific situations or events in their lives. Personal traumas such as illness, the loss of loved ones, "recovery" points where the last drink was had or the last cigarette was smoked, all trigger responses which often scream out for acknowledgment. It is beyond the intent of this book to discuss these reactions in any depth, as they do not constitute celebration, per se. However, a useful guiding principle is that personally significant days should be recognized rather than left bottled up in the recesses of one's unconscious. Too many individuals expend too much energy fending off the powerful feelings associated with difficult historical moments, rather than allowing the healing which almost always comes from granting expression.

I have been deeply touched over the years by the ways people have found to acknowledge difficult anniversaries. While visiting grave sites may not be for everyone, a middle-aged male client, who lost his younger brother in a car accident when they were in their twenties, wrote a poem each year to his departed sibling. He would visit the cemetery on the anniversary of the accident, recite the poem, and experience what he called a deep feeling of connection with his brother. A woman who was in recovery from alcohol abuse would spend the anniversary of the day she took her last drink at a homeless shelter, gently trying to find a way to get in touch with individuals who were losing themselves to alcoholism or other substance abuse.

◆ Graduations ◆

While graduations are not exactly holidays, they do mark personal transitions, from grade school all the way through college and professional school. It is also clear that the months of May and June are colored by young people in gowns and tuxedos being transported in family cars and, in some cases, very long stretch limousines. Celebrations of graduations are often two-pronged events involving first, a family gathering and second, the big night with the graduates' peers. Since there is no universal way to celebrate these propitious days, it is not always easy to negotiate the form the parties will take.

To the dismay of most parents, the central issue often boils down to how alcohol will be managed— considering that its consumption has become deeply associated with coming of age in our culture. This problem is most pressing for the parents of high school graduates, since the legal drinking age usually exceeds the students' age by at least two years in most states. In the last few years, everyone seems to have become more sophisticated with respect to handling this inebriation anxiety which, unfortunately, can overshadow the actual basis for the celebration. Schools provide bus transportation to senior proms, and parents routinely ask their children's guests to turn in their car keys at home celebrations. This unfortunate overemphasis on drinking as the cornerstone of graduations has caused much conflict, and in some cases tragedy, when rules have not been followed. Operating on the fringes of what is lawful, disagreeing with the emphasis on ritual drinking, and worrying about events becoming uncontrollable all make for a very uncomfortable affair. As a society, we have much to learn about how to both resist adolescent pressure to celebrate in this way, and to examine our laws and values which have reified the role of drinking in this vulnerable period of early adulthood.

This discussion of drinking detracts from the real

essence of graduation, which combines a sense of leaving behind with that of moving on. During their junior year in high school, most ambitious students begin to realize that there are choices to be made in the not-so-distant future. The sense of leading "programmed lives," divorced from the pressures of making responsible decisions, gives way to a feeling that there is now much at stake. Grades, teachers' evaluations, extracurricular activities, sports participation, and those dreaded SATs all begin to intrude into the carefree perspective of the adolescent. Apprehension about choosing the next educational path, worries about finance, plus the simply overwhelming array of choices, make this a very stressful period.

Still, graduation from college is probably more difficult. There is the same set of worries about creating a job resumé, in addition to another set of examinations, should postgraduate studies be a consideration. However, the greater pressure at this point has to do with being able to make what could be lifelong commitments to a vocation or continued training in professional school. The achievement of ego identity discussed in the previous chapter really comes into play here, as it is excruciatingly difficult to confront these decisions in the absence of a developing sense of who one is.

Few contemporary college graduates seem to have a definitive sense of where they fit. It has become increasingly popular for college graduates to return home, often to the dismay of parents who have become accustomed to their own independence. The same lethargy and lack of direction portrayed by Dustin Hoffman in *The Graduate* seems just as relevant today. While graduating is certainly a cause for celebration, it is important to accept and understand the anxieties that are often just beneath the surface.

◆ *Vacations* ◆

Vacations are opportunities to break away from the routines of everyday life. They do not involve special meals, greeting cards, or pressures to exchange gifts. Yet vacations often elicit the same blues patterns as other holidays. Some people actually dread vacations because they require actively planning what to do with "unstructured" time. Individuals or couples may become so entrenched in their work-day routines that they find themselves out of sorts when faced with figuring out what to do with time that is not part of their life program. "Workaholics," in particular, become anxious as soon as their work routine is threatened. That is not to say that most individuals do not jump at the opportunity for a paid vacation. The trouble begins for many when choices must be made about where to spend that time, and how.

I recently worked with a female client who refused to go on vacation with her husband until he made some serious changes. She claimed that his approach to a vacation was to load the trunk of the car with legal briefs, his computer equipment, and "the straw that broke the camel's back," his fax machine. A male client complained that his wife could not be without her cellular phone; whether they were at the beach or on the tennis court, she insisted that her staff could not function without being in touch with her. The new generation of communication equipment certainly reinforces this kind of self-defeating approach to vacation.

Vacation behavior can sometimes be a microcosm of how individuals approach life in general. At different stages of life, we have the feeling that "time is flying," and find ourselves powerless to slow it down. Generally speaking, people with the most crowded calendars experience time as getting away from them. To slow down that sense of time passing too quickly, they need to allow for periods of non-goal-directed activity. Vacations are obvious opportunities to get off the treadmill and live from moment to moment. However, this change in pace creates initial anxiety, and does not occur without strong deliberation.

People become amazingly conflicted about how much to structure their vacation time. On the one hand, there is the tendency to plan lots of interesting activities. On the other hand, we spend our day-to-day lives living by the clock, so that on vacation it is desirable to "play it by ear." A balance obviously needs to be struck. If we make no plans, it is possible the vacation may come and go with a sense of boredom rather than replenishment. Yet, conversely, if too many activities are planned, the vacation will race by like our routine life, with little sense of definition or rest.

It is common to hear couples say that they need to get away in order to renew or enhance their relationship. This is obviously a good idea whenever possible, but things do not always turn out as expected. Some of the worst crises have occurred when couples who are having difficulties go off on holiday with expectations for reparation. Busy couples who have serious relational difficulties often mask them as they live their customary lives involving careers and family. However, when they realize that they cannot effectively communicate, or when sexual expectations are not met, the discomfort level triggers conflict which couples may be unable to manage in the absence of their usual "escapes." I have had couples return from vacation with the sad realization that a long-term relationship was in serious trouble, or at the point of no return.

Simply spending time together is not an antidote for relationships full of unresolved conflicts, without the joint capacity and commitment to make progress before letting a holiday work its magic.

Missed Holidays

Due to the particular dynamics of contemporary life, many individuals find it difficult to celebrate a variety of holidays. Relocations, divorces, and remarriages, as well as inter-ethnic marriages, have caused a need for inventiveness with respect to celebrating in meaningful ways. Some people may find themselves alone in new communities, while others are not accustomed to supplying the energy to celebrate when they separate from marriages or family. Men who get divorced are especially vulnerable, as they have often depended on their wives and/or children to provide the work and context that goes with holidays. Co-parenting couples struggle with orchestrating holidays or changing schedules of having their children from year to year: one year one parent has a child for Thanksgiving, and the next he/she does not. The same can be said for all holidays that are shared, often after an acrimonious process of negotiation. This pattern of alternation seriously conflicts with the maintenance of tradition which, after all, is at the heart of celebrations. Often the parent who is having the "off year" struggles to find a meaningful way to celebrate, since he or she may not be linked to a particular context.

Co-parenting, of course, can work successfully. Halloween, in particular, seems to allow for a brief merging of separated families even when there has been considerable conflict. Perhaps because "trick or treat" occurs on neutral ground outside the home, it is possible for divorced parents to join their children for an hour or two of cooperative parenting. I have worked with a divorced couple who actually turned Halloween into a tradition of mingling stepfamilies. The annual celebration was not only beneficial to the children but also seemed to improve the communication between the divorced parents.

Both remarried and inter-ethnic couples find themselves having to accommodate or negotiate what can be relatively foreign patterns of celebration.

When individuals remarry, they often do not realize that there may be a difficult adjustment in terms of the traditions to which they have been accustomed in their prior marriage. Obviously, the longer the previous marriage lasted, the more established their holiday patterns might have become. It is not always apparent when couples are dating just how each approaches holidays. In addition, if they have not been exposed to each other's families, they may find that the joys of a new relationship can quickly become compromised when they encounter new, and possibly foreign, traditions.

Even the simplest of activities can lead to unanticipated difficulty. A couple in their late 50s ran into a problem concerning the issue of when to open Christmas presents. They came to see me after being married only two years, certain that they would never be able to weather another holiday season.

The man, whose children were grown and living in Europe, felt strongly that "Santa was long gone" and he was accustomed to opening gifts on Christmas Eve in front of the fireplace. His new wife, who had three grandchildren living nearby, was used to the more conventional approach—opening presents on Christmas Day, so that the children could indulge in the Santa fantasy. Though feelings ran very high, their problems did not extend much beyond this gift-opening conflict. The roots seemed to be in their prior marriages, where both had become accustomed to yielding to overbearing, dominant spouses. When the couple realized they were bringing past relationships into their new marriage, they easily found a way to compromise. They opened their presents on Christmas Eve, and focused on the children on Christmas Day.

A more difficult issue is associated with people who are not part of a social group, and don't have the luxury of negotiating a holiday celebration. They may find themselves disconnected from friends and family, and have to face the problem of how to survive another holiday alone. This predicament occurs for a variety of reasons, ranging from divorce to relocation or a more complex pattern of behavior that has led to social isolation. Clearly, some individuals have personalities that tend to preclude much social involvement. On the surface, it seems that this group should not mind celebrating in their preferred social mode: alone. Others, however, yearn for an invitation which never seems to come, and find themselves "on the outside, looking in."

As extended families have dispersed, there seems to be fewer and fewer automatic holiday celebrations. Twenty or thirty years ago, a holiday such as Thanksgiving would not be associated with much travel. Now, it is the most heavily traveled week of the year, with highways and airports filled with individuals working their way to a distant point of celebration. There has also been a breakdown in continuity, with no center of the family. As so many grandparents have relocated to the South or Southwest, they have ceased to be the mainstay of holiday celebrations. I have heard so often that spending the winter holidays in Florida "just doesn't feel the same."

Whatever the factors that contribute to "missing holidays," this situation is capable of eliciting a variety of blues patterns. In the next chapter, two particular isolation patterns will be examined which are closely associated with spending holidays without other people. The surprising aspect of this phenomenon is that we are not talking about hermitic or reclusive individuals exclusively. Some of the individuals who come to mind function quite well in the non-celebrative part of their life, which is usually work. However, when society stops for its intermittent pauses, these individuals always seem caught short, and can't wait for the pause to end.

Holiday Blues Profiles: 3
Are You a Grinch, A Loner, a Merrymaker, or a Lost Soul?

Blues patterns do not exist in a vacuum. Holiday behaviors are usually symptomatic of tendencies that manifest themselves in other aspects of day-to-day life. For example, the tendency to become anxious when attempting to accomplish things to an unrealistic standard will affect all aspects of life. When someone becomes frantic at the thought of preparing a holiday meal, or choosing the perfect Christmas gift, that same exacting behavior is likely to be present when he/she is at work, on vacation, or at the supermarket.

This perspective is particularly important when it comes to the daunting task of trying to undergo a serious campaign of change. Some other works on the subject have suggested that a few well-placed inspirational directives have the power to alter established patterns of behavior which are rooted in the personality of individuals. While I have witnessed some rapid alterations in functioning, it is wise to be patient with holiday blues, as the change process may be slow as well as threatening.

Since people tend to have favorite holidays as well as problematic ones, we must look at both factors in attempting to create a useful summary of holiday blues patterns. As with psychological disorders, the focus here is on the problematic behavior patterns that are usually bothersome to individuals. However, it is not entirely true that all blues patterns are objectionable to those who possess them. Thus, as you examine these profiles, you may or not find yourself within the descriptions. Individuals vary greatly in their levels of self-awareness and openness. By the same token, be careful in attempting to apply labels to others, as they are not always delighted by the prospect of getting unsolicited feedback. As with most psychological habits, it really helps when people ask for your help.

The eight blues patterns I have identified are broken down to three groups, based on the predominant emotion governing the behavior. While these emotions do not occur completely to the exclusion of other feelings, it is useful to look at problematic holiday profiles in terms of Anxiety, Sadness and Depression, and Frustration and Anger. This grouping should be especially helpful when confronting the question of alteration. When we are able to see the connections between behavior patterns and underlying emotions, the prospect for positive change is greatly enhanced.

Anxiety

Anxiety is a universal, painful feeling, which we all experience from time to time. It can keep you awake at night, cause problems with concentration, and wreak havoc with basic physiological processes. Anxiety is often associated with headaches, hypertension, and digestive problems, in addition to psychiatric disorders, such as phobias and panic attacks. Due to the pain associated with anxiety, we attempt to reduce it through various psychologoical defenses, as well as using chemicals, which range anywhere from from prescription drugs to illegal, mood altering substances.

When we are very young, we feel anxious when separated from our parents for the first time, being forced to trust a stranger to care for us, for a given amount of time. That same kind of separation anxiety is felt when changing schools and going away to camp. As we grow older, we begin to feel anxiety about our performance in our various societal roles. This can be the nervousness that comes with the knowledge of an impending exam or that of wanting to hit a home run in your neighborhood league's weekly game. By the time we reach adulthood, our anxieties can be triggered by less direct factors, such as our desire for social approval or our inability to formulate a set of workable life goals. Holidays can be a catalyst for anxiety as well as the result of self-defeating patterns of behavior.

As we will see in the following groups, the onset of holidays arouses anxiety in certain individuals. The patterns of behavior, which characterize their approach to celebration, end up compounding their anxiety. Resulting in their feeling upset and unfulfilled.

◆ *The Juggler* ◆

This is the prototypical holiday blues pattern in that it covers so many occasions and fits so many individuals. This person always approaches holidays with "too many balls in the air." When holidays appear, there are simply too many perceived obligations and responsibilities, and the stress level begins to escalate. The Juggler's natural tendencies seem to be counter-productive. He/She does not delegate very well, and, in the face of mounting stress, will intensify the effort to get everything accomplished. No matter how busy life gets, the standard does not shift; all the presents must be bought, the cookies baked, and the house decorations cannot be compromised. The Juggler usually pulls off a pretty good celebration, objectively speaking. The tasks get done, and the "production" aspects of the holiday are usually accomplished without any of the balls being dropped. However, this blues profile exacts a toll on the Juggler, in particular, and on everyone around him/her. By the time the holiday is over, everyone is relieved because the holiday is not fun and potentially not meaningful.

Each year as Christmas approached, Carol, a 42-year-old mother, wife, and attorney, got caught in a familiar pattern of spiraling anxiety. In fact, although she really cares about holidays, any which required some preparation made her feel anxious. The problem is that Carol cares about everything else in her life with equal intensity, and has the tendency to believe that a bright, successful, and conscientious person should be able to attend to all facets of life without compromise. She is always on the go, with time being the main enemy in her life: there is simply not enough of it. She takes on too many projects, in addition to her work outside the home, her family responsibilities, and the myriad social obligations she tends to accumulate. Not surprisingly, she has described herself as trying to be "Superwoman."

Because of the protracted nature of the Christmas holiday period, Carol spent sleepless nights worrying about achieving all the goals on her holiday agenda. In fact, on several occasions she actually felt better when she got out of bed at four in the morning and "did something." Though physically exhausted by this process, she was somewhat relieved at actually wrapping some presents, baking some cookies, or writing out her endless list of holiday cards. During the Christmas frenzy, Carol's moods would swing wildly, from energetic and positive to depleted and anxious. Inevitably, these moods would impact on her husband and children, who actually came to dread the holidays.

What is most fascinating about these patterns is how they occur despite high levels of intelligence and strong negative feedback from family and friends. The Juggler creates a sense of chaos around her so that others cannot figure out how to participate or assist in the holiday preparations. According to Carol, her husband would become somewhat passive in the face of her activity level, and her two teenage children would follow suit. She would accuse them of being passive-aggressive, and fights would often follow. On one occasion, things got so out of hand that she and her husband actually had a physical altercation, for the first time in their marriage of 21 years. Talk of divorce followed, and both children took the side of her husband, who moved out of the house for the two weeks before Christmas. He came back in time for the actual holiday because of a strong sense of duty to his children and to his extended family.

Carol started therapy immediately after this dramatic holiday season. She was astounded that she had never realized how unhappy her family was in the role of observers of her holiday hyperactivity. A reasonable question, which should come up in any family where one member is engaging in extreme behavior, is whether there is "co-dependency" in the sense that other members encourage or support the problematic behavior. One might ask whether Carol's husband's passivity was instrumental in evoking and sustaining her high level of isolation and anxiety. While such dynamics are often relevant, it was not the case in this family. Carol's juggling pattern predated her marriage and seemed to be the force that rendered both her husband and children observers. They were, in fact, delighted that she decided to start therapy, and willing to participate in the process. Carol became aware that her approach was self-defeating, counterproductive, and antagonistic to the essence of the holiday she was trying to celebrate. What astounded her most was that she did not have this insight until she brought her marriage to the brink of disaster. She really believed that what she did was for others, and that they loved and admired her for her tireless juggling act, and was shocked to learn just how unpleasant the holidays had become for her family. Eventually, Carol was able to see just how painful the season had become for her, as well. The Juggler commonly functions as somewhat of a martyr who believes that what he/she does is good for others, even if they do not realize it. Consequently, he/she is always surprised to find that their anxiety and level of activity creates guilt and resentment in the people around them.

As Carol's therapy progressed, we discovered that the juggling pattern had affected the people who worked with her in her law practice. She had a difficult time keeping assistants, and younger colleagues did not seek her out as a mentor. After some inquiry at her office, she discovered that her hectic pace and perceived chaotic way of working frustrated people and engendered feelings of failure, much like in her family. This revelation shocked Carol, whose perception of herself was that she was always trying to please everyone else. In fact, she felt as if she were living in a kind of "time warp" where there was never enough time for anything. She juggled in order to seek success in all domains of her life—a pattern that is familiar to many working mothers.

Professionals, in particular, whose work schedules are indeterminate and demanding, find themselves doing an exhausting balancing act between the requirements of career and family. They race from activity to activity feeling anxious, out of control, and often on the verge of "wanting to drop out." To some degree, the Juggler blues pattern is a symptom of our modern hectic lifestyle, in conjunction with a certain personality profile that seems predisposed to get caught in this trap. However, the Juggler is someone who is operating at the far end of the continuum, and often lacks the insight or flexibility to take corrective action on his or her own.

◆ The Perfectionist ◆

The Perfectionist personifies the anxiety state, striving to make all endeavors in life reach a standard that is usually unattainable. There are two basic types: one who is able to achieve his or her goals, and the other who, after intense effort and deliberation, simply cannot be pleased with an accomplishment. As with all blues patterns, there is always a continuum of behaviors to be considered. The person who simply has high standards for holidays or any other aspect of life is not the target of this book. The Perfectionist profile concerns the level of dissatisfaction this individual brings to himself/herself or to other celebrants. It does not seem to favor either gender, as the holidays are torturous for an equal share of men and women. The meaning of holidays quickly fades as celebrations become "productions" on which one will be judged by an unspecified and imagined audience of significant figures.

Mike was a successful, 52-year-old real estate developer who had amassed a tremendous fortune through a combination of hard work, perseverance, risk taking, and a self-proclaimed ruthlessness in his business affairs. Every year, he would throw a lavish New Year's Day party at his home, a sprawling country estate with horses and vineyards.

His reason for choosing this time for a party was revealing in itself, as he was sure that most of his acquaintances would not have anything to do that would compete with the event he created. Moreover, he had held the party for 15 consecutive years, assuming that everyone would plan to attend on an automatic basis. One of Mike's concerns was that there not be a high turndown rate and, in fact, if people did not RSVP in a timely way or did not attend for a few years, they were dropped from his list. Each time he planned the party felt like the first to him; no detail could be left unattended, for he was determined to make the occasion unforgettable. He was fanatical about the specifics of the catered menu, and although this was supposedly his wife's domain, he oversaw and was critical of her every decision. Equally important was the music, which ranged from exotic Middle Eastern dancers to classical ensembles to jazz trios to choral groups. He was particularly ruminative about seating arrangements, preoccupied with hearing "lively dialogue" while making sure that he and his wife were able to circulate among their guests in a fluid way. While Mike's annual gathering did not quite make the social page of the local newspaper, it had become well known among a certain social group, who talked about it for weeks afterward. Sadly, their comments were often disparaging, least of all the evaluations made by the host himself. Some guests joked about the "overdone" quality of things, and about how hard Mike tried to impress a social group who seemed indifferent to his efforts to join them.

Mike grew up on the fringes of what he perceived to be the most affluent and powerful social group in his community. While he attended private schools and went onto an Ivy League college, his parents were shopkeepers, unlike his friends' fathers, who were bankers and entrepreneurs. According to his wife (his third), Mike was viewed as something of a social climber, and did not receive many reciprocal invitations despite the effort he put into his annual gala. In fact, she claimed that they fought continuously over their lack of social acceptance, with much of the blame being directed at her. She feared that their marriage, like his first two, was destined to fail if he did not develop some perspective on his self-defeating pattern of attempting to win approval from a loose assemblage of people who seemed to have little interest in him. One of the most defining aspects of Mike's life was his failure to gain membership at a social/athletic private club with a reputation for selectivity and a history of "blackballing." He was constantly astounded that, despite the strong representation of club members at his party, he was not encouraged to reapply.

As one could well imagine, preparations for the New Year's Day party were little fun for Mike's wife and children. He was anxious for weeks beforehand, and as the event approached, he became critical of their plans, himself, and even the extraordinary setting. His family felt that the entire holiday season was compromised, even ruined by his self-centered focus on winning approval. Probably the worst part was that Mike was never pleased by the outcome of the party, but would slip into a "blue" state during the weeks that followed. As is often the case with obsessive individuals, the product of their labor is never good enough, and they focus on minor imperfections, or even invent them when there are none. Mike came to see me in the aftermath of one of his parties, searching for a way to recreate a sense of the holidays for his family, who were on the verge of mutiny. The situation was coming to a head as his children became teenagers and began rebelling against their father's perfectionism.

Mike was ready for some major changes in his life. He was ready to examine his "earnest" approach to everything he did as he realized that it was a losing strategy. He became aware that he did not have real friends, and was on the verge of alienating the only people who really cared about him, his wife and children. He claimed that the turning point came during a conversation about the holidays with a house painter who was working at Mike's in preparation for the party. Mike says he realized how this "simple working guy" was looking forward to his holidays, and how relaxed the painter seemed when discussing his plans for an annual party—the very thing that tortured Mike.

After many years of overdone extravaganza, Mike decided to cancel the party and replace it with a brunch for his immediate family and the few people he considered close friends. We discussed this shift in therapy over and over, until he felt that the anxiety about being "socially relevant" would be worth getting over. The main theme in Mike's therapy was his overwhelming need for approval from others, which he traced to an overemphasis on appearance which had plagued both his parents. His mother, he recalled, was most critical of him, and always had something to say, no matter how he behaved or looked. Another important revelation had to do with the subtle ways his mother blamed his father for their lack of acceptance in the community. As Mike's holiday blues were deeply embedded in his personality, therapy was not able to bring about a complete change in him. His critical behavior towards himself and others was not completely discarded, and his strident tendencies were not amenable to change. However, to his delight, his holiday pattern was altered as he found that the wisdom of his house painter was an unanticipated, very valuable gift.

Striving for perfection can ruin a holiday, especially if the person is surrounded by others who do not share the same tendencies and, in fact, are annoyed by what they perceive to be rigid behavior. Nancy was a recently married Jewish woman who had temporarily retired from her career as a speech pathologist to raise her daughter. She had been raised in a religious household, where dietary laws were followed and holidays celebrated along traditional lines. Though her husband was also Jewish, he was raised in a less observant household in which holidays were acknowledged through traditional foods and an occasional appearance at the synagogue.

After her father passed away, when she was 30, Nancy offered to hold Passover dinner at her house, and expected that her husband would lead the Seder, as is the custom in traditional households.

Nancy described herself as a very organized and conscientious person who liked things in her life to be structured. She was that way as a student and in her career, and tried to manage her household that way. She claimed that she was like her father, an accountant who, according to her recollection, was really a Perfectionist. He and her mother argued about money and being on time. She remembered that at Passover, things had to be just right or "there would be hell to pay." Since the Seder is meant to be highly structured, with an abundance of colorful ritual, many observant Jews feel that there is a "right" way to conduct it. However, there is tremendous latitude in interpretation of its structure. Some families conduct the meal following the rules of the prayer book in a very literal way and try to maintain a serious decorum, while others interpret the holiday as an average American family would celebrate Thanksgiving. For the latter family, there might be loose attention to the religious protocol and a much greater emphasis on having a good time, and enjoying the novel foods.

Nancy was determined to celebrate Passover in a way that, as she said, "would have made my father proud." She planned to follow traditional guidelines to the letter, and put all her energies into buying and cooking foods she recalled from childhood. She focused on creating the perfect meal, attempting to match an internal picture of how every thing should look and how the evening should progress. In the weeks leading up to Passover, she became highly anxious and irritable.

The problem began as it typically does for Perfectionists, who either assume that others share their high level of anxiety or that they have been made sufficiently aware of how they must support the Perfectionist's exacting standards. Nancy's husband agreed to lead the Seder, but was not prepared to maintain the serious tone of the meal for himself, his children, or his family. The result, as one might expect, was somewhat of a disaster. His brothers who were in attendance had a habit of joking throughout the meal, and did not pick up the growing tension as Nancy kept trying to restore decorum to the meal. She looked to her husband to little avail, as he became increasingly drawn into the holiday behavior with which he was most familiar. He grew distracted and annoyed as she began whispering in his ear, chiding their children, and noisily removing the complex sequence of plates and flatware required throughout the meal. Eventually, toward the end of the meal, she "lost it," left the dinner table in tears, and refused to return. The rest of the family hastily finished the meal and, with little fanfare and great self-consciousness, withdrew from Nancy's house.

It is difficult not to feel sorry for Nancy, and to take issue with her husband and his family for not taking her efforts more seriously. If there must be a right and a wrong, clearly she was the hostess, she did the lion's share of the work, and she attempted to maintain a family tradition. How could one argue with setting a high standard for the celebration of an important religious holiday? The problem with Perfectionists' approach to holidays, and everything else, is that they often "miss the forest for the trees." They become so focused on getting things right that they lose the significance of what they are attempting to achieve. Anxiety keeps them from perceiving situations clearly, and from making the best judgments. We could certainly raise issues about Nancy's husband's lack of empathy and his brothers' insensitivity. However, her focus on details without reference to others diminished the likelihood of her plans reaching fruition.

Like all Perfectionists, Nancy tended to be self-centered, and lost sight of the needs of her family and guests. As she came to realize in therapy, her anxiety to make things perfect was not really directed at the people with whom she shared the holiday. Rather, she was unconsciously trying to please her recently deceased, highly critical father. After considerable work in therapy, she understood that the problem was not with the high standards she set, but with the ineffective way she communicated her expectations to others. After skipping one Passover celebration, she tried again, this time with more favorable results. Her husband attempted to get his family to treat the experience with more reverence, and she tried to be more flexible as the inevitable mistakes were made. Perfectionists have a tendency to ignore the compromising efforts of others. They can appear spoiled, as their anxiety interferes with their ability to appreciate that others are trying to be accommodating. Nancy's anxiety did not go away altogether, but was helped by the relatively successful experience she was able to orchestrate. The Perfectionist does not give up easily!

◆ *The Merrymaker* ◆

Just as the Perfectionist tries to live up to an impossible standard as a way of dealing with anxiety, the Merrymaker tries to live up to an internalized image of what a holiday season should entail. On the surface, Merrymakers are those people who really know how to celebrate. Their key concept of holidays is indulge, indulge, indulge. This pattern is probably most evident around the end of the year because of the extended opportunity for celebrating. The key to whether someone is simply having a wonderful time or is a victim of a blues pattern can often be detected in the aftermath of a holiday. In a sense, the Merrymaker is like an individual with a bipolar disorder who, after being in a manic phase, will often "crash" into a depression in a very cyclical manner. In the same vein, the Merrymaker often becomes morose after an extended period of overindulgence and can actually end up depressed, with a real case of the post-holiday blues.

Anxiety plays a role for the Merrymaker in two ways. First, it energizes him to approach the holidays in a frenzied fashion. In addition, hyperactivity itself can trigger more anxiety, so the person gets caught in a vicious cycle. Virginia, a 36-year-old history professor at a small college, came to see me shortly after the new year with a very compelling story. She and her husband, a successful and flamboyant stockbroker, had a tradition of celebrating the Christmas season by attending as many cocktail parties as possible. The season was typically a blur, as they were caught up in what appeared to be a vague sort of competition with known and imaginary rivals. This pattern went on for about 15 years and, according to Virginia, had its roots in their dating years. They attended the same college, which was known as a "party school," and Virginia took some pride in portraying them both as definite "party animals".

As adults, when they became settled in their community, they began to attend elaborate functions at country clubs, or lavishly catered holiday parties. Over the last few years, according to Virginia, she began to drink much more than usual at these events. At one memorable pre-Christmas party, she had been flirting with a male friend who attended with his wife, also a friend. Their mutual heavy consumption of alcohol led to a romantic encounter in a remote part of the club, and in the process of "fooling around," Virginia's dress was torn so severely that she could not return to the party. The male friend ran to get her coat, so that she could cover up and make an excuse about why she needed to abruptly leave the gathering. In the meantime, her husband had gone looking for her, and a staff member who had noticed the couple stealing away pointed him in their direction. In true sitcom fashion, her husband and the other man approached Virginia at the same time. While her attempted explanation might have reached a credible threshold, the other guy anxiously stumbled his way into apologizing, thus giving away the real story.

Virginia and her husband went through a predictably difficult period as a result of her recklessness. The worst part, according to her, was the embarrassment as rumors began to develop into inventive "coatroom" stories. Most striking for Virginia was the degree to which she and her husband seemed to be stuck in this pattern of overindulgence. It was actually he who first began to acknowledge that their immaturity had been making him uncomfortable for some time. Neither of them knew how to initiate a major shift for fear that the other would cease to be attracted to the one who broke their pact of "eternal youth." It was not easy for this couple to change, as their identities and their perception of social acceptability were tied up with the Merrymaker routine.

Many individuals who have trouble with alcohol revert to problematic patterns around the Christmas season, and often encounter difficult circumstances. A 45-year-old engineering project manager actually got himself fired at an office Christmas party. After drinking heavily and using cocaine in the men's room, he relentlessly tried to seduce a much younger woman who reported to him. Though he was a valued employee with no history of inappropriate sexual behavior, the young woman was so upset that the firm thought it was in everyone's best interest to part company with him. Sadly, this man admitted that he had gotten into trouble at other office parties, but had always been forgiven for his excesses. He had to learn the hard way that the culture we now live in is much less tolerant of irresponsible social behavior, not to mention the possibility of endangering others by getting behind the wheel of a car.

In addition to substance abuse, the holiday season becomes a license for individuals to overindulge in all kinds of ways. Certainly this applies to eating excesses, as attested by the popularity of New Year's resolutions which are attempts to apply behavioral brakes. Some Merrymakers actually begin to diet just so they may binge when holiday time comes. Another area of excess has to do with spending money, especially around Christmas. This particular phenomenon might be considered a pre-blues pattern, in the sense that the real trouble begins when the bills begin to arrive after the new year. Many people go into so much debt as a result of holiday spending that they spend the rest of the year paying down their Christmas bills. Unfortunately, many who do not manage to get their bills paid end up in dire financial straits.

Merrymakers often feel great remorse after the holidays. The "eat, drink and be merry" approach can leave them in a wake of trouble, with considerable repair work to be done. They may experience feelings of self-loathing due to the repetitious aspects of their behavior, as well as some sense that the "spirit of the holidays" was violated. Merrymakers tend not to be reflective by nature, so that there is an inclination to fall back into old patterns as the memory of past mistakes is lost. However, when these people get into trouble with alcohol, health, relationships, work, or finances, they may be able to summon the necessary energy to seek help and address their problematic behavior patterns. The point is that without a major, self-motivated attempt to redefine the meaning of celebration, changes will be superficial and short-lived.

In order for Merrymakers to make lasting changes, it is necessary to confront their personal identities, the psychological sense of who they are. Ultimately this redefinition and the related shift in values provide the fuel for the change process. Often, because overindulgence is associated with sin, there can be a desire to shift to a more spiritual or religious way of viewing both life and celebration. That is probably the reason that self-help groups such as Alcoholics Anonymous infuse a combination of spiritual and behavioral parameters into their programs. The point is that without this major self-motivated attempt to redefine the meaning of celebration, changes will be superficial and short-lived.

Sadness and Depression

Unlike other holiday blues profiles, this one begins with a sense of being "down" at the very outset or anticipation of celebrations. Holidays become triggers for these people whose lives are out of balance in some way. Sometimes, it is a clear-cut sense of social disconnection, while at other times it has more to do with a feeling that their lives are simply not in order. Holidays can be thought of as magnifiers that illuminate our relationships to our families or other significant social groups. Sad or depressed people tend to dread holidays because this amplification process becomes associated with the pain of facing strong feelings that can be ignored at other, less significant times. Birthdays, long summer weekends, religious holidays, and most certainly the winter holidays can all stir feelings of sadness and/or depression. Key holidays simply cannot be avoided. When businesses and schools close down, when the entire culture transforms itself into celebration mode, it is not possible to sidestep holidays. It is even difficult to avoid the more personal milestones, although there are often no external cues or pressures to acknowledge them. Though some individuals say they discount birthdays or anniversaries, if they are sad or depressed, it becomes very difficult to hide from themselves and others.

◆ The Mourner ◆

As the name implies, this is someone who experiences celebration with a sense of grief and regret. This person acts as if he or she is dealing with a loss rather than the positive anticipation of a holiday. The question, of course, is what has been lost? The Mourner, for the most part, has a tendency to live in the past, with a sense that nothing in the present measures up against childhood memories. They have a very difficult time with their current life. Whether through divorce, occupational disappointments, or natural calamities, sometimes our present life is simply inferior to the past.

Imagine, for example, how Kosovo refugees might have felt the first time they had to celebrate a major holiday in a strange land with few familiar people, surrounded by alien traditions. That is not to say that we all do not, and perhaps should not, yearn for some of the feeling from our more carefree past lives. On the contrary, sentimentality is what provides the impetus for the continuity of tradition. Mourners do not actively try to recreate and build on their positive memories of a prior time; rather, they feel despondent and tend to dread the onset of milestones that remind them of the past.

The grief reaction to impending holidays is not always based on negative present circumstances. Many of the Mourners I have known seem to be living reasonable lives with all the possibilities for enjoying their celebrations. Nevertheless, they lament about how they cannot get the desired feeling that they recall existed in their wonderful childhoods. Closer examination, however, often reveals that their childhoods were not always so splendid and, in fact, were sometimes dreadful. The past that is being longed for may be glorified or idealized, rather than the perfect recollection that is the basis for experienced Mourners. As a defense against toxic memories, people often reconstruct and distort the painful aspects of their histories. In particular, children who have been hurt or disappointed have the capacity to fantasize about their celebrations in order to maintain hope and optimism. As adults, these individuals often cope by avoiding anything that evokes the feelings they work so hard to defend against. Holidays, then, are potential sources of forced memory. It is sometimes more comfortable to feel melancholy and nostalgic about the idealized past than to deal with the painful repressed memories of childhood.

Initially, Mary's husband Stephen came to see me because he was tired of having spent more than 30 years watching Mary yearn for her childhood every Christmas. Stephen met Mary in western Europe shortly after the end of World War II. He had been stationed there, and they met at a church dance when she was 17 years old. After a brief courtship, he was reassigned to the United States. In spite of a twelve-year age difference and her deep attachment to a large extended family, Mary's parents gave her permission to marry Stephen and emigrate to the United States.

Mary has a good sense of humor and a charming style. Her early years in the United States were difficult, but she was soon excited by "the openness of the people, and the freedom to be who you want." She and Stephen had two daughters within four years. Mary said that she had been happy, despite missing her family.

But each year, at the beginning of December, Mary would become morose and melancholy, and essentially refuse to participate in the upcoming holidays in a positive way. In her case of the blues, she deviated from being a basically upbeat person, and became depressed and unhappy. Recalling that this pattern began after the birth of their second daughter, she explained that having children put her in closer touch with her memories from Europe. She began to long for her family and their traditions, which were quite different from those of the "commercial" American holiday.

Initially, Mary was resistant to discussing her childhood memories of Christmas. She claimed that the vagueness of her memories was due to terrible associations with the Great Depression, the rise of Fascism, and the outbreak of World War II, in which she and her family lived in a constant state of terror. She spent some time touching on painful memories of Nazi occupation, and events that such a life circumstance evokes. However, it was actually a recurring dream that revealed why Mary was reacting to each holiday season with such a profound sense of mourning.

The dream involved images of her as a child, but dressed as a flamenco dancer in a sexy black costume with a red rose in her hair. It was a complex, convoluted dream, from which she awoke with a start when an "elderly gentleman" approached her. As is often the case, she kept making references to this dream until, in a session two months later, she remembered a terrifying night with a great uncle who had visited her family during the difficult period before World War II. After some difficult sessions, following powerful eruptions of buried emotion, it was clear that she recalled childhood sexual abuse over an unclear extended period of time. Her recollections of this period were associated with the holidays.

Thus, we discovered that Mary's adverse reaction to Christmas was not really based on longing for splendid childhood experiences; on the contrary, she used a psychological defense to idealize her childhood, and avoid some very painful experiences. Mary did not change her holiday reactions overnight. It was very painful to realize that a lifelong set of behaviors was based on suppositional events, with no characters around to support or invalidate her new "theory" of herself. After recovering this terrible memory, Mary finally got through one Christmas without the usual mourning reaction. She was determined to stop making her American family pay the price for the horrors of her childhood.

Mary's case was more complex than that of other Mourners. Some individuals are indeed responding to drastic life changes involving economic or family factors. For example, growing up in comfort, and then having to struggle as an adult, can be very difficult.

Jay, a 42-year-old automobile salesman, had what he called a "perfect childhood." He had grown up in a rural section of Virginia. Extended family members were close, and lived within 25 miles of each other. Jay described his life as trouble-free all the way through college. He was a good athlete, had an easy time socially, and did not recall any difficulties from his youth.

Holidays were usually spent with maternal grandparents who had a large house, a great deal of land, and a small lake where Jay, his younger brother, and cousins spent countless hours fishing and playing. Jay recalled warm, harmonious memories, doted on by energetic and caring relatives in a "picture postcard' setting. He went to an out-of-state college on a football scholarship. There he met his wife, who was, according to Jay, the most sought-after cheerleader. They were married during his senior year, and after graduation moved back to Virginia, where Jay went to work in his father's retail business. It was shortly after returning home that Jay's storybook life began to change.

His marriage, which he later realized was based on superficial factors, quickly became problematic. His wife, who wanted to be a fashion designer, did not adjust well to a rural lifestyle, and was uncomfortable with what she felt was a controlling family. She did not like the "automatic" aspects of their holidays, and wanted to be more independent than Jay or his family was ready to accept. After a year and a half, they separated; she went back to Atlanta and Jay continued to work in the family business. Around this time, Jay's grandparents' health began to decline. First his grandmother developed congestive heart failure and died within six months. Shortly after, his grandfather had a severe stroke and had to be placed in a full-care nursing home. To help pay for the extensive cost of medical care, the "family homestead" was sold to real estate developers, who turned Jay's childhood haven into a townhouse community. To make matters worse, Jay's father's business began to degenerate as chain stores came into the area. His father decided to sell out to a national chain. After a year of feeling lost, Jay took a job with a new car dealer and began to establish a degree of independence.

Eventually, Jay remarried, and his second wife, Diane, persuaded him to move north so that she could complete an educational program not offered in the region where they lived. Jay was successful in his new career, but had never quite gotten over longing for his idyllic childhood. His attitude toward holidays was to try to ignore them. Diane went along with this, especially while she was in the throes of her master's degree program. However, after she graduated, they had their first child, and she began to expect the usual holiday celebrations. Everything she arranged with her small family or new friends just upset Jay, for nothing could compare to memories of holidays at his grandparents' farm. She tried to create meaningful celebrations, while Jay took on the demeanor of a detached observer mourning for another place and time.

Diane was remarkably patient in that she did all the holiday planning and tolerated his passivity with good humor. Jay remained in this non-productive grieving pattern until he went on a fishing trip with his younger brother. It was his brother who helped Jay stop yearning for a past that was interfering with the possibilities of his present and future. It seems that his younger brother had followed the same path of lamentation to the point of causing a marital separation. Jay was moved by the similarities in their perspectives, and decided he would not allow his second marriage get into trouble. To Diane's shock, Jay offered to take charge of the next Thanksgiving meal. He invited everyone he could think of. With some guidance from the therapeutic process, he took care to avoid recreating the exact meal or customs on which he had been so fixated for all those years.

This yearning for the past represents a basis for depression. Mourners have to let go of glorified memories of another time, and channel their energies into the possibilities that exist in their present life.

◆ *The Loner* ◆

This is not the stereotypical image of a person who is reclusive and has no connection to the world; that individual is more likely to have serious mental health problems related to his or her detachment from the world. Our Loner is often male, and can actually give the appearance of being rather social. Usually, he is deeply involved in his career. The Loner generally has a fair amount of acquaintances, keeps a busy schedule and, on the surface, appears to be quite content. One might think of the driven executive or the traveling salesman as the personification of this blues pattern—a pattern which, incidentally, seems to have become more prevalent over the past few decades.

Our cultural predilection for allowing our careers to define us tends to support this syndrome. Many people, male and female, migrate to large business centers such as New York, Chicago, or Boston, and throw themselves into their jobs. It is not uncommon for them to work 12-hour days, six or seven days a week. This immersion in work appears to create the illusion that they are socially connected, with many solid relationships. However, the connections seem to vanish, and Loners can suddenly feel invisible, wishing that a given holiday would be over as soon as possible.

Tom is a 45-year-old business consultant who spends most of his time traveling. Affluent and divorced, Tom never developed a close relationship with his 19-year-old son, blaming it on the rigorous travel schedule he had maintained for many years. Once his son had started college, they saw each other less and less, with most of their contact limited to the weekly phone call. Holidays for Tom were focused mostly on his son, with whom he would manage to connect briefly when his son was not with his ex-wife. Tom had a brother and sister, but they had also grown distant as they lived in other states. His relationships with them were defined by impersonal greeting cards and occasional phone calls.

Tom claimed he had friends, but, as he explained when he began therapy, "everyone is involved in their own life." Like many Loners, Tom projected a self-contained image, so that no one ever thought to see how he was faring. He carried his professional demeanor of confidence and self-assurance so convincingly into his personal life that his golf buddies never thought he might need a place to go on holidays. Tom also managed to keep his romantic relationships at arm's length. He dated several women, but was fond of saying that he made it clear he was not open to getting "too involved." Consequently, his female friends also assumed that when holidays arrived, Tom was busy with undefined family matters.

Tom was raised in a family that placed great emphasis on achievement. He was quick to joke about his father as a "relentless taskmaster" who only paid attention to what you didn't accomplish. Despite graduating from an Ivy League school with a B.A., and a well-known university with a M.B.A., Tom felt that he had never received enough recognition. Consequently, he was able to connect his driven work life with his demanding family. He grew up feeling that he did not need to count on anyone, and tended to equate closeness with "neediness." This attitude was costly in his marriage, where his wife became fatigued with "seeking him out." After 17 years of marriage, she met another man and asked Tom for a divorce. He remembered responding, "I guess you have to do what you have to do."

After his divorce, Tom found himself spending all major holidays alone. At first, he rationalized with the thought that it gave him time to "recharge," and get caught up on his work. He also comforted himself by expressing the cynical view that holidays were "Hallmark inventions" anyway. He tried to believe that he was quite comfortable letting holidays slip by. The event that triggered his therapy was a Thanksgiving when his son had an opportunity to spend the four-day break with a classmate in Florida. Finding himself with no plans, Tom began to panic and question his "Loner" approach to life. Suddenly, he became maudlin about the holidays, to the point that he had detectable anxiety episodes with each passing occasion.

Tom had to do a lot of work in therapy to change his Loner status. His whole identity was tied up in his work and independence. To become more emotionally connected with his son, Tom arranged a long weekend with him so he could begin to shift their relationship. Though his son was resistant to the change at first, eventually he agreed to a more structured approach to holidays, which involved the recognition that Tom needed him and wanted to share the "corny holidays" when time permitted. Tom had a more difficult time forging a committed relationship so that, in his words, he and his new girlfriend could begin to "get a life together." At first, he worried that his productivity would suffer, but as time went by, he was able to see that by meeting some of his human needs, he felt more effective in his work, traveled less, and worked fewer hours.

Jan, an unmarried, 52-year-old television producer, had come to find the winter holidays excruciating. For many years she had kept busy with her career, producing shows in exotic settings and mingling with celebrities from all fields of the entertainment industry. She described her holidays as "non-events," and viewed celebrating Christmas or Thanksgiving as something that "ordinary people" did. Particularly when she was younger, she tended to sneer at family get-togethers and saw herself as more of a free spirit who had no time or inclination to do what other people did at holiday time.

Jan grew up in a middle-class, religious family in the Midwest. Her father, an insurance broker, was very dominant, and ruled the household with an iron hand. Her mother was a housewife who managed to keep the family from being completely morose, despite their obvious unhappiness. Jan claimed that she realized later that her mother gave her and her two sisters strong covert messages about making sure they got to use their talents and, above all, not to be dominated by a man. In other words, "Do what I suggest, not what I do." Whenever the inevitable fight broke out between her parents, Jan would watch in pain as her mother yielded to her father, while seeming to give her three daughters the message, "Don't allow yourself to get into this position."

Jan attended a women's college, became deeply involved with the women's movement, and read a great deal of feminist literature. She dated men throughout high school, college, and afterward, but was always careful not to get too attached. She resisted bringing boyfriends home to meet her parents, and avoided becoming involved with her boyfriends' families. Jan was not especially articulate about her motives, but when she was younger, she was simply uncomfortable in a traditional female role. In her relationships with men, she felt that she needed to assert her equality and seriousness of purpose so she would not be misunderstood. In retrospect, Jan said she might have "come on too strong and chased some good guys away." She claimed it didn't matter, since she had never wanted to get married or have children.

As Jan approached 50, she began to tire of her lifestyle. She began to travel less, and was less enchanted by the glamour of the media business. For years she had convinced herself, her family, and her friends that she was not sentimental, and did not need to have special days acknowledged. Yet she felt very badly when her fiftieth birthday went by unnoticed except for a few humorous cards. She did not send greeting cards, and the only presents she had ever bought were for her niece, the daughter of her divorced youngest sister. Jan had worked so hard to be independent that others believed she did not need to be included. Perhaps, more important, she had convinced everyone that she did not want to slip into complacency by wasting time and energy celebrating "mass-minded" holidays.

Jan's therapy was not about a serious change in her lifestyle. Nor was she about to revamp her philosophy about holidays, and suddenly join what she called the "regular folks." Instead, she needed to affirm her choices, and understand them in the context of her current life. She needed to put her career in perspective, accept that she had fashioned her life as a Loner, and make the most of it. With respect to holidays, she decided she had spent too many years waging a costly protest against the subjugation that she associated with family life. She began to realize that she could allow tradition into her life, on her own terms.

◆ *The Lost Soul* ◆

The Lost Soul's defining trait is the pervasive feeling of "poor me." Unlike the Loner, the Lost Soul tends to maintain his or her holiday stance in most other aspects of life. He/She lacks optimism, and perceives a holiday neither as a celebration nor an opportunity for general goodwill, but as just another life situation in which he/she will not perform well. The Lost Soul tends to live life in a ponderous fashion, with general feelings of inferiority, avoiding situations in which a risk of self-expression will have to be taken. Self-pity often governs the Lost Soul's life, resulting in a failure to accomplish even the most unambitious goals. Because procrastination and resentment are characteristic, holidays are experienced as intrusions and distractions. Gifts and cards are sent late or not at all, resulting in a vicious cycle of poor performance and self-devaluation.

Barbara, a 49-year-old computer technician, originally began therapy because of problems she had with men. Soon after her divorce, when she was 41, she began a series of disappointing, short-lived relationships that lacked substance and usually dissipated after a few dates, which were, she complained, merely "excuses to get me into bed." Barbara was reasonably successful in her career, and had risen to a middle-management level in a large health care company. Despite her outwardly successful appearance, she had a dreadful self-image, both in terms of her appearance and her social relationships.

Barbara described herself as a "perennial outsider, always looking in at other people's lives." She had always felt excluded from life's special occasions. High school proms, spontaneous outings, and even phone calls from friends were not part of her adolescence. Growing up, she never had a best friend, and was not close with her two older sisters, whom she felt treated her as an annoyance. To this day she feels alienated when it comes to sharing her life. Her parents never took a great interest in Barbara, and she felt she had basically raised herself. Though there was no known history of depression in her family, the mood was certainly depressive in every respect, with each daughter leaving home as soon as possible after graduation. Holidays were not memorable, but Barbara recalls her mother lamenting that things were "never right," that they never received the right invitations, and that she resented the burden of holidays.

It was sometimes difficult for Barbara to tell whether she was being ignored by the world or she was pushing everyone away. This question of cause and effect is really central for the Lost Soul. In other words, one must ask: Am I perpetuating the experienced exclusion from childhood, and am I aware of that process? Inevitably, the only useful way to think about this situation is to assume that certain behaviors do trigger others' reactions, but that the Lost Soul is not really aware of how this happens. Barbara was not aware of the many ways she turned off people. She was generally negative, wore a scowl on her face, and had a very difficult time with generosity. She felt and acted like the proverbial victim. Eventually Barbara came to see how she actually chased people away with her demeanor and negative outlook on life. In her own words, she knew she was a "downer."

Breaking this vicious cycle is not an easy matter. The combination of low self-esteem and fundamental distrust of others is deeply embedded in the personality of the Lost Soul. This emotional foundation, coupled with a set of unattractive social behaviors, is difficult to breach. Years of stinginess, complaining, and bitterness take their toll on the relationships in a Lost Soul's life. With Barbara, the change process was slow and intermittent. She did not know how to be positive, and learning to change her outlook was not simply a matter of changing attitude. The shift from a Lost Soul blues pattern was a serious psychological risk for Barbara. To become a participant in celebration would mean taking new risks, for optimism is predicated on trust in people and hope in the future, and Barbara had neither. After several years of therapy, her successes have begun to outweigh the setbacks.

Gary had been in recovery for more than ten years before he sought psychotherapy. He had managed to successfully control a drinking problem, developed during his college years, by a deep immersion in Alcoholics Anonymous. He attended at least one meeting a day, which he claimed helped him avoid the terrible memories of his days as a serious binge alcoholic. Since his recovery began, he had taken over a small family retail business, keeping his life as simple and predictable as possible. He met Sandra at one of his AA meetings, and they were married soon afterwards. Their life was uncomplicated and highly structured, revolving primarily around their busy AA meeting schedule.

Together, Gary and Sandra built a wall around themselves, and were generally satisfied that they were no longer drinking. They avoided social events, particularly parties, and gradually withdrew from the few friends they shared. When holidays arrived, they tended to make excuses, supporting each other's stated wish to stay home and not deal with the complexity and temptation of holiday celebrations. Though they could take pride in overcoming their mutual substance abuse problem, both were beginning to slip into a malaise brought on by an overemphasis on their "one-day-at-a-time" lifestyle. They attended a few family gatherings, but rarely made plans, and never organized any social functions of their own.

Gary and Sandra's life took on a colorless quality. The simpler it became, the more they resented having to extend themselves in any way. Gary likened his feelings to a leg that has fallen asleep—you know you have to move it, but you dread the feeling it will cause. One year he noticed that they were being invited to fewer and fewer family celebrations. At first he and Sandra had taken solace in not being invited. They actually felt that people were being understanding of their "sheltered" lives. They both continued to attend AA meetings, and watched a great deal of television in their considerable spare time.

Their change process began when, for the first time, they found themselves alone on Christmas and New Year's Eve. Family members with whom they had celebrated in the past had decided to spend the holidays in Aruba, and anticipating Gary and Sandra's reaction, did not invite them. It is likely that years of disinterest had caused resentment in those family members. Not being included had a powerful effect on Gary. At first, his reaction was the predictable "poor us" attitude. However, when he discussed the problem at one of his daily AA meetings, an old trusted friend suggested that Gary rent the movie *Dead Poets Society* and pay attention to its main theme. Shortly after contemplating the significance of "carpe diem" (seize the day), Gary decided to start therapy.

Strongly identifying with the character played by Robin Williams, he decided to stop feeling sorry for himself and "get off my couch." He proclaimed that he was sick of his boring life, and that he was going to be active and "take some risks." Although Sandra did not share his enthusiasm, Gary still pursued his goal of embracing some new relationships. One of the women he "embraced" turned into a romantic relationship. This new liaison, coupled with Gary's sustained motivation to stop functioning in a "lost" fashion, changed his life. Sandra was not up for a major change, and seemed to retreat deeper into her shell in response to the changes in Gary's personality. As often happens, when change does not occur in a mutual way, a relationship can become threatened. Gary and Sandra eventually divorced, with an awareness that sometimes couples can provide the wrong kind of support for each other.

Frustration and Anger

The last pair of blues patterns are quite interesting because they involve the same kind of emotional reaction expressed at two different points along the holiday continuum. In other words, while the Grinch reacts with irritation and anger at the hint of a holiday, the Fixer seems to approach each celebration with a renewed sense that all the imperfections of the last occasion will be remedied this time around. Another way of understanding these individuals is to note that they are the ones who spoil holidays for other people. They either rain on the parades of others' attempts to celebrate with them, or they simply manage to generate enough tension to take the significance and pleasure out of just about every holiday.

◆ *The Grinch* ◆

We all know and do *not* love the Grinches, who can also be called the Scrooges. They seem to bring to life the characters depicted in Dickens' *Christmas Carol* or the perennial Christmas TV cartoon, *The Grinch Who Stole Christmas.*

Impending holidays put Grinches into a bad humor, as if they will be forced into a behavior or situation incompatible with their sense of themselves. Grinches are more common than one might imagine; in fact, most of us can probably identify at least one in our nuclear or extended families. Their negativism can range from a passive-aggressive refusal to participate in holidays to an almost evil capacity to spoil everyone else's good times.

The passive-aggressive Grinch is often male, and tends to half-heartedly go along with holidays. Gifts are often given late, sometimes with a promissory note. Last minute shopping or preparations are common, and he rarely fails to let you know how far out of the way he had to go to fulfill holiday expectations. Grinches tend to be forgetful, often invoking such explanations as, "You know I never get into holidays." One of the most upsetting tendencies associated with this forgetfulness is the failure to follow through with commitments.

Robert was always in charge of buying wine for a lavish Thanksgiving dinner at his home. More often than not, he would completely forget to do it, or buy the wrong type or quantity of wine. Needless to say, this annual "mistake" wreaked continuous havoc with his wife's holiday preparations.

A variation on the passive-aggressive Grinch is the person, again often male, who has "ideological" problems with various holidays. The complaint is either that the holiday contradicts the essence of its true meaning, or he simply says, "I don't believe in these corny celebrations." The trouble with this type of Grinch is that he never seems able to find the right way to celebrate. Instead of negotiating with family members to adjust holidays to his ideology, he seems to thrive on attacking convention, much the way rebellious adolescents try to define themselves by rejecting tradition while still being intrinsically linked to it.

Angry Grinches are the most unpleasant. They are the spoilers. Their aggressiveness and irritability make it impossible for anyone to celebrate in their presence. Even holidays that are oriented toward them evoke a problematic response. They express annoyance when their birthdays are acknowledged, frequently return gifts, and can be quite disruptive if anyone dare to surprise them with a party. There can be no holiday where the expectation is harmony, for angry Grinches manage to leave behind a wake of hurt feelings and holiday disappointment.

Hal, a 52-year-old banker, had gotten away with being a Grinch for his entire married life. He and his wife Camille lived in a fairly typical suburban community. Camille and their three children had developed a remarkable tolerance for Hal's holiday irritability, and basically celebrated all occasions by "going around him." He removed himself from holiday preparations, while Camille managed to create structure and tradition for the children by tapping into relatives on important occasions. Thus, they always went to Hal's parents' home for Thanksgiving, and to her mother's for Christmas. Camille attended Catholic church services at Easter and Christmas with the children while Hal, predictably, stayed away.

Camille had managed to survive Hal's Grinch behavior for 27 years by "keeping a stiff upper lip," and by an increasingly caustic sarcasm concerning his level of detachment. She insulated their children from Hal's toxicity, making her jokes to other family members and anyone else who needed her to "run interference." The trouble began when Hal's oldest daughter married into a traditional Christian family who celebrated the full range of holidays with gusto and pride. Now Hal's Grinch repertoire would have to be explained to a new set of people who neither shared his history nor the tolerance of his loved ones. Conflict was avoided at the actual marriage, as both sides agreed to a small, family-oriented wedding, and offered funds to the new couple for a "nest egg" instead of for a lavish event. Soon after their marriage, however, the parents of Hal's new son-in-law invited him and his family to Thanksgiving dinner. Hal was immediately uncomfortable, and began to exhibit his usual behavior in an attempt to escape from this new holiday situation. That is when a major family disturbance erupted, bringing his Grinch routine under extreme pressure.

When Hal's newly married daughter broke the silence, and began to confront both her father and mother, the seeds for change were sown. Their daughter, having gotten some new perspective from observing her new father-in-law, and feeling the support of her husband, said she would not participate in her family's weird habit of "enabling" her father anymore. She and her father argued, then stopped speaking. It was Camille, however, who erupted in a major way, venting years of frustration over spoiled celebrations and personal deprivation. She threw down the gauntlet by proclaiming that she and the two other children would attend Thanksgiving dinner with or without Hal.

It was actually Hal's daughter who began therapy, because she was feeling profound conflict. Her family physician had recommended psychotherapy when she developed a severe skin rash. After a few sessions by herself, first Camille, then Hal, were brought into therapy with her. Though it was difficult, Hal grudgingly began the process of understanding and tackling his negative holiday behavior. It was very clear from the outset that his Grinch posture was rooted in an adolescent rebellion that never really started. Hal came from a fairly typical and traditional family that went through the motions of holidays. Though somewhat unusual, it was Hal's mother, not his father, who turned out to have been somewhat of a "closet Grinch." While his father plunged into each holiday in a structured and predictable way, his mother never seemed to have her heart in it. In fact, she was generally uncomfortable with much of their life, which Hal came to realize in the therapy process. She was not a strong enough personality to alter their approach to celebrating, but her subtle sarcasm seemed to provide a foundation for Hal's later cynicism. Because of his father's strong personality, Hal never openly rebelled against holidays or anything else. He was a grudging conformist who pretty much went along with the educational and social programs expected by his father.

Hal developed what one might call a "counter identity." He was clear on what he was against, but had no real perspective on his own values. He did not manage to go through a constructive identity crisis in late adolescence. In fact, it seemed that he spent his adult life under the influence of his mother's unexpressed rebellion, stuck in adolescent negativity. The task for Hal, or anyone caught in this counterproductive psychological position, is to tackle the business of developing a positive set of values. Not surprisingly, that task was threatening for Hal, as it meant giving up his needling and making a commitment to a life perspective that he could defend. His therapy was filled with stops and starts as he tried to apply his cynicism to the process. On two different occasions, he stopped treatment, but came back with a promise to continue to work on an "adult identity" which would allow him to let the Grinch die away.

Grinches, as we have seen, are not always males. Jan, a 34-year-old piano teacher, had grown up in a small New England town with her mother. Her father, who died when Jan was eight, had not left a significant amount of money for the two of them. Despite being surrounded by extended family, life was difficult, and her mother worked long hours as a private nurse. Jan remembered spending a lot of time alone, worrying about her mother's health and the bills which her mother "never stopped talking about." She was extremely frugal, saving most of her baby-sitting money and, like her mother, wearing clothes that were either handed down from a more affluent aunt or bought at a local thrift shop. Jan was a serious and diligent student who put herself through a small regional college with a combination of scholarships and student loans.

In her senior year of college, she met Scott, a first-year veterinary student at a nearby university. He came from a wealthy family that had fallen on hard economic times during his adolescence. Though he was in the same boat as Jan, he spent money more freely, and frequently "maxed out" his credit cards. They married shortly after Jan graduated and found a job teaching music in an elementary school. From the beginning of their marriage, they fought about money. They disagreed on how much to spend on their honeymoon, their first apartment, and their car.

Celebrations magnified their differences. Jan continuously chided Scott not to be extravagant on her behalf. Inevitably, he did not listen, and bought her presents at fancy retail establishments, as opposed to the discount stores where

Jan always shopped. She would end up returning most of what Scott gave her (except the flowers), and he would look disappointed when he opened her gifts. This pattern prevailed in all aspects of their lives. If they were invited to a wedding, they argued over the value of the gift to be given. If they were able to agree that they would take a vacation, Jan questioned Scott's choice of accommodations. In the final analysis, they tended not to take holidays unless she made the arrangements.

By the time Jan was 30, Scott was established as a veterinarian and earning a solid living. Nevertheless, the same dynamics persisted, except that the gap between them was widening. Scott now felt that he had regained some of the economic stature he had as a child and wanted to express it. Jan, dumbfounded by the amount of money they were spending, became increasingly frustrated and angry as she felt she was losing control of their financial life. She wanted to maintain a frugal lifestyle, and save for the proverbial rainy day. Scott responded to her Grinch-like attitude by becoming defiant. Instead of lavishing her with gifts on their anniversary or her birthday, he began treating himself to better cars, "toys", and clothes.

The irony of the situation was that Jan's assessment of their economic situation was not completely invalid. Their level of debt increased, though Scott tried to justify it by claiming that they "needed more tax deductions." The worst part of the situation was that the more Jan became a Grinch, the less she liked herself. Eventually, she understood that her negative approach to holidays, and to life in general, could threaten their marriage. She questioned why she was always the one to put the brakes on their spending. She managed the money, paid the bills, and dealt with the anxiety over meeting tax payments and monthly cash flow. Jan actually described herself as cheap, boring, and a spoilsport.

The question was how to break the vicious cycle of her anger and Scott's indifference. Jan realized that she wanted to let go of the fears associated with her childhood. To succeed in shifting her emotions about holidays, she would have to detach herself from the burden of managing their money. After some difficult negotiations, Scott agreed to take over their family finances, and Jan agreed to do two things. First, she would stop overseeing Scott's spending habits and disapproving of both his excesses and his generosity. More importantly, she made a commitment to suppress her irritation and learn to accept the role of celebration in her life. Jan proclaimed that she would know that she was no longer a Grinch when she neither asked how much a gift cost, or if it had been purchased on sale.

◆ *The Fixer* ◆

The Fixer seems to have a very short memory. At each "sensitive" holiday, this individual conjures up hopes for how he/she is going to change irritating, long-standing personal or family behavior patterns. Every year, the Fixer approaches the holiday with renewed expectations to alter disappointment, with a familiar result: frustration, anger, and a failure to enjoy the holiday because of the failure to change anyone or anything at all.

The art of celebration can and should have a place for modification and evolution. The difficulty for the Fixer is that he/she seems to have the same agenda year after year with very unhappy results. In fact, when hearing the stories of Fixers who end up frustrated and angry after each holiday, one gets the feeling that the more they try to "fix," the less things change.

Bruce, a 41-year-old small business owner, had been married twice, and had two teenage children from his second marriage. Bruce grew up in the Midwest, where his mother and two older sisters still lived and ran a successful family advertising agency. Despite what he considered his best efforts, he was unable to convince them to travel and celebrate holidays with his wife and children on the east coast. His mother always claimed she wasn't "well enough to travel," and his sisters always had a reason why they couldn't break away from their busy lives in the city where they grew up. In fact, only once in 15 years did they actually agree to celebrate Thanksgiving with Bruce, his new second wife, and their young child. The result, he recalled, was awful. His mother spent much of the time exhausted in bed, and his sisters and their children complained about how Thanksgiving just wasn't the same away from home. Naturally, this left both Bruce and his new wife seething about the shoddy treatment they experienced at the hands of his family.

After that visit, Bruce resumed his annual trips to see his family in the Midwest, with resentment building each year. To make matters worse, his mother had an upsetting habit of bragging about her other grandchildren, making Bruce and his wife feel like second class citizens. Several years before I met Bruce, he had tried to become an "activist" in his family. Based on a therapy group to which he belonged, he decided to confront his mother and siblings. The trouble with his attempt to fix the family dynamics was that he always tried to do so during the holidays, with poor results. His mother would end up crying, his sisters and their husbands would get angry, and Bruce would go home vowing never to visit again. Each year, he seemed to forget, and would work himself into the same expectant state before returning to the predictable arena of his family.

Very often, the frustrations felt by Fixers are valid, and the observations they make about what needs fixing are accurate. The problem is that they stir resentment in the rest of the family, who may or may not have the same complaints about the character of their holiday celebrations. In many respects, Fixers get a reputation for being spoilers, so that the family actually digs in its collective heels in response to what they perceive to be annoying behavior. In addition, the dynamics that trigger the Fixers' reactions are deeply rooted in a family's history, and are not easily amendable to change.

Bruce grew up in the shadow of his older sisters, one of whom was a gifted athlete and the other immensely popular. He seemed to be adequate, but his deceased father had been disappointed when Bruce chose not to join the family business. His mother seemed unprepared to be involved with a son, and therefore Bruce had a long history of feeling much less acknowledged by his family. They seemed to place a great emphasis on public affirmation, which made Bruce and both of his wives extremely uncomfortable. His nieces and nephews followed the family blueprint, while his children were viewed as merely adequate, with few exceptional accomplishments to report to their grandparents. As with many Fixers, frustration and anger at holiday time are really rooted in historical patterns that become magnified during the crucible of a special dinner. In fact, Bruce recalled that when he was in his early teens, he dreaded the dinner hour, when he would have to listen to the endless success stories of his sisters, to the beaming delight of both parents.

There are many vexing family patterns to which Fixers respond. Families who eat in a flash and spend the rest of Thanksgiving watching football on television are certainly a target, as are those where long-standing tensions erupt around the dinner table. Bruce's annual feedback on where he stood in his family is repeated over and over in different contexts and in different ways. Many people complain that they feel ignored, invisible, or inadequate in the context of family celebrations. The urge to "fix" is a constant source of conflict; the results are usually self-defeating, and perpetuate the cycle of frustration and anger.

The key to breaking this pattern is for the Fixer not to attempt to make an impact at the actual holiday. Instead, the time between holidays should be seen as an opportunity to approach any amenable family members who could become allies. Bruce discovered that one of his sisters actually had a complaint similar to his. Although she obviously did not share his objection to the family tradition of celebrating holidays in the Midwest, she was able to relate to the discounting of his children, especially by their mother. His sister explained to Bruce that she had noted this divisive habit some years ago. Their mother always seemed to talk about "whoever was not the focus of a conversation." In other words, if his sister mentioned an accomplishment of one of her children, her mother would either talk about her other sister's family or even Bruce's children. Bruce was amazed at this revelation. He and his sister began a dialogue that allowed them to formulate a joint strategy for the holidays. Eventually, the other sister was at least willing to entertain the notion that their family was less than perfect, and did what she could to spread goodwill around. While none were really able to have a productive dialogue with their mother, their awareness of the dynamics helped reshape the tone of family gatherings. This new connection to his siblings was quite powerful for Bruce, and he was able to diffuse much of the irritation he associated with the holidays. Ironically, as he identified less with the role of "spoiler," his sister managed to convince their mother to celebrate the next Thanksgiving on the east coast, at Bruce's house.

Techniques for Surviving the Holiday Blues

4

Ten Commandments to Help Improve the Quality of Celebration

The daunting problem for blues sufferers is that they seem to get blind-sided in the face of their particular holiday nemesis. Each year, they either find themselves automatically drifting into their pre-holiday pattern, or in some unexpected noxious state on the heels of a holiday. The skill they seem to lack is a sufficient amount of timely self-awareness. The ability to "know thyself" is valuable, in general, and indispensable when it comes to avoiding self-defeating holiday patterns. Undoubtedly, anyone who suffers at any holiday should be able to identify, at least in part, with some of the individuals whose lives have been briefly described.

The first element in this process of self-assessment is to be able to find yourself within the constellation of blues patterns. Try to recognize your dominant tendencies, bearing in mind that the categories are essentially an outline. In practice, these few "pure" patterns are comparable to a diagnosable physical illness. A Mourner may also have the qualities of a Loner, while a Fixer could also be somewhat of a Perfectionist. By the same token, dividing up the responses by dominant emotion is also somewhat artificial. An individual who experiences anxiety often experiences sadness and/or frustration at the same time. Finally, to make life really interesting, different holiday occasions might elicit different feelings and blues patterns. The same individual might be a Juggler around the winter holidays, but just like a Lost Soul around the summer holiday, depending on his or her life circumstances.

The importance of identifying problematic holiday patterns is that you can work on your behavior, independent of the holiday itself. This is particularly crucial if there are to be significant changes in holiday experience. By the time a holiday is upon us, anxiety, sadness or anger has been evoked, causing a decline in the ability to productively alter oneself. This ability to anticipate the "dangerous" holidays is not easy for most of us. Once you have survived an ordeal, there is a tendency to sigh with relief and put that particular holiday out of mind. But before you know it, it's holiday time again, and you repeat the same unsatisfying repertoire as in the past.

One might question whether it's possible to change

self-defeating behavior without professional help. People do in fact change old habits, addictions, and routines all the time. With or without the existing plethora of self-help books, individuals successfully give up smoking and drinking, and have varying degrees of success changing their eating habits. Others, often after life-threatening experiences, make radical changes in their priorities. After a serious heart attack, one man gave up a demanding executive position in advertising to become a clerk in a department store. The fact is that many people make all kinds of changes on their own, based on all kinds of internal prerogatives. Someone who decides to leave an unproductive and painful relationship can also demon-strate the ability to make self-induced changes.

However, it is also true that many individuals do not have the tools to make changes on their own. Poor persever-ance, lack of insight, and insufficient motivation can com-bine to make any significant change process less than likely. Also making change difficult is the fact that some of the blues patterns I have discussed are rooted in people's personalities. The Lost Soul, for example, may have a tendency to be de-pressed. In the same way, a Perfectionist at holiday time may have that tendency with all tasks, making the prospect of change rather daunting. In some cases, appropriate psy-chotherapy may be the best approach. The type of therapy will depend on the nature of the problematic behavior. Holiday patterns that can be seen as somewhat isolated bad habits might be best treated with recently developed behav-ioral therapy approaches focusing on the bad habit itself, without probing into any underlying factors. The laws of learning and conditioning can be applied over a few months to help break behavior patterns.

Blues patterns that are connected to values, personality problems, or family conflicts, or are driven by unconscious historical processes, might be better treated with the depth psychotherapies. A Grinch, for example, may need to find a way to shift his values in a more affirmative direction. The exploration of those values might best be done in what are called the humanistic or existential therapies. When holiday blues patterns are embedded in complex family relationships, therapy can focus on parts or the whole family. This approach is often termed systems therapy, because the goal is the modification of relational dynamics. A Mourner who is disturbed by historical memories might best be served by entering into a more classical form of psychoanalytic therapy with a focus on the unconscious issues from the past.

Whether a person commits to a program of self-directed change or seeks professional help, there are some universal concepts that should provide a focus for the successful confrontation of blues behavior. Since I have already pointed out that holiday blues patterns are not always pure, the tools for change are not organized specifically according to personality type. Thus, rather than suggest a "cure" for each holiday malady, my Ten Commandments for improving the quality of the holiday experience are presented in terms of recommended shifts in behavior or psychology. Each commandment will probably be more applicable to one or two holiday patterns than all the rest. However, it is best to consider these concepts as a set of universal principles, to safely guide you through the treacherous waters of problematic holidays.

The Ten Holiday Commandments

1. Embrace the Holiday Essence

Advice to stay true to the meaning of a holiday may seem self-evident. Despite the fact that holiday celebrations ought to relate to the cause for celebration, it does not take much consideration to realize how far we stray from the true significance of holidays and, worse yet, how often we cannot even find a rationale for the celebration. If you are not convinced, try a simple experiment. Ask people you know socially or at work to describe the origins of Halloween, Valentine's Day, Christmas trees, or eating potato latkes during Hanukah. It is astonishing how detached we have become from the meaning of our celebrations, and how we both blame and allow ourselves to be controlled by commercial forces.

One might rightfully ask how it could relieve the holiday blues to be more cognizant of holiday essence. So many problematic behavior patterns during holidays concern such clearly peripheral things as gifts or overindulgence. Emphasis and re-emphasis on the meaning of celebration takes energy and conviction. Every December parents, as well as religious leaders, implore us to downplay the commercial aspects of the season, and the material frenzy that often overshadows all other aspects of the holiday. These voices are ignored, mocked or, in most instances, patronized. It is not fun to be the parent who limits the number of gifts given to her children, or to insist that some time be devoted to acknowledgment of the holiday essence. Children, especially, thirst for this kind of tradition, since they are more detached from intergenerational influences such as grandparents, uncles, and aunts.

Because so many families are not strongly influenced by religion, the responsibility for shaping holidays falls on individuals. Many attempt, especially at Thanksgiving, to infuse the holiday with more *personal* meaning than simply eating a meal, by stating what they are thankful for. Though they may be reluctant at first, family members can gradually relate to a new ritual until it becomes part of their annual celebration. Of course, Thanksgiving is easy since there are no gift exchanges, and parties are confined to a family food fest!

Christmas is the holiday that raises the most conflict and evokes the majority of blues patterns. When voices speak against the commercialization of Christmas, they often go too far, limiting their audience to a few courageous zealots. The rest of us pay some lip service, and then manage to get caught in the powerful seasonal tide. There are many techniques for making serious inroads during this period. For Christmas, it is a straightforward matter of getting in touch with the spiritual aspects of the holiday. Apart from actual religious observance, theologians with whom I have spoken have isolated some themes that probably have relevance for our entire culture. Since Christmas has become a winter break for most of our culture, the opportunity for a "shift" is important. Time off from work or school provides a perfect opportunity for either travel or simply hanging out. Especially for the fast-paced family, this season can provide a chance to move at a more leisurely pace and engage in activities that are not time-pressured—for example, ice skating, winter picnics, and exploration of the natural and cultural opportunities that one can find or make anywhere.

Hanging out becomes an important tool for dealing with anxiety, especially for the Juggler and the Merrymaker. In my research on temporality, it became clear that the time warp these individuals experience around holidays is positively affected by activities which are not timed, and certainly not squeezed into a busy schedule. That is why the crafting of gifts, which can range from highly skilled projects to home-baked simple holiday cookies, can be very satisfying. Another important aspect involves the opportunity to spend more time with people who are significant in our lives. The expression "quality time" has become overused as we try to offset the complexity of our lives. However, it is not only external factors that keep us from having these elusive times together. Our own personalities and habits are the main factors that prevent us from the interpersonal nourishment we seek. Quality time is not like food on a menu; it cannot simply be ordered. Relationships must be sustained over time with energy and creativity. Holidays simply give us extended opportunities to talk, play, solve problems, and venture into new terrain together. We have the option of relating to major holiday themes while deepening our connections that we cherish.

For each holiday, we should pause to reflect on why we are buying a gift or planning a special gathering. Above all, we should be sure to communicate our understanding— or our questions—to those around us. This conveying of meaning is especially important to children, who soak up all such information with wide, innocent eyes. This substantive pause itself is not a corrective technique for overcoming the holiday blues; rather, it provides a compass to help steer us through significant shifts in our celebrations.

2. Exercise Choice

We often hear people say, "I hate birthdays," or "Valentine's Day is just another opportunity for the greeting card and flower industries." The surprising thing is just how many of us essentially go through the motions on certain special occasions. There are two primary choices we need to make with respect to celebrating holidays.

The first choice is whether we acknowledge and celebrate at all! While this sounds radical, it is far better to spare oneself and others from Grinch-like behavior. So many individuals want to confront the Grinch and say, "Why don't you simply not participate or just stay away completely and leave the rest of us to enjoy the holiday?" The fact is that Grinches are often powerful family members such as parents, and the behavior goes on year after year. The idea of confrontation is one thing, but actually breaking into longstanding family patterns is pretty daunting.

In a sense, then, the choice about how to deal with holiday negativism belongs with both the perpetrators and the "victims." The best solution, of course, would be for the angry individuals to become reflective and make their own choice about how to deal with their anger. These turnarounds do happen, but often after people lose patience and refuse to participate. It is really important for those who experience anger or frustration during the holidays to first accept that the behavior, in fact, occurs; and, second, to explore why it persists. The reasons for such behavior are often rooted in historical factors. Sometimes it is the simple imitation of someone from the past or a defensive measure to deal with fears. Holidays, as we have seen, dredge up a whole continuum of feelings ranging from sadness to fear.

A woman I worked with years ago had the insight that she became "bitchy" around Christmas as a way to control her Merrymaker husband. She somehow developed the habit of becoming negative as an unsuccessful way of "keeping my husband's spending under control." She managed to ruin her own holidays this way, and was ironically not effective in reshaping her husband's spending habits.

When we consider the option of exercising choice to overcome holiday blues behavior, it is critical to remember that choices are made all the time. When we think of habits, good or bad, we sometimes forget that we have the freedom to affect what we do at all times. The problem is that so much of our behavior seems automatic, when in fact there is so much room for greater personal control. The trouble with holiday behavior is that we go on autopilot, and do not feel we are exercising choices along the way. As a psychologist, I am always working with the ambiguous link between conscious and unconscious influences on behavior. The task for individuals, with or without professional help, is to make our behavior intentional so that we can assume full responsibility for how we behave.

Sometimes our behavior is based on conflicting needs, which confuses individuals as well as others in their lives. Anthony had a very difficult time with both his birthday and Father's Day. He was divorced, and always found himself "stewing" after these two holidays. Somehow his grown son and daughter never seemed to acknowledge the days with enough thought. They would send cards, but often late, and the presents were "token" when they were sent at all. Upon closer examination, Anthony discovered that he behaved in a decidedly aloof way about these personal days, especially before his divorce. He saw himself as "the provider," and was always saying,

"Don't buy me anything—there's nothing I need." His former wife apparently saw through this ruse, and usually did the appropriate things on these particular days. His children, however, took him literally, and believed that their father did not care about receiving gifts because he wasn't sentimental. Getting Anthony to exercise the choice of honest self-assessment and direct communication with his children turned out to be, in his children's words, "totally refreshing."

In addition to whether we celebrate a given holiday, there is the even larger issue of how we celebrate. So many people who suffer through holidays get stuck in a pattern that they feel they cannot avoid. They allow their past or other individuals to shape their approach to the holidays. There is room for tremendous creativity, especially when it comes to making key decisions about the approach to celebration On the one hand, there is the understandable desire for continuity and maintenance of tradition. After all, tradition is the mainstay of most holidays. To reinvent each celebration would be too cumbersome, and might actually detract from the significance of the occasion. Instead, we need to be ready for self-diagnosis, to see what pattern has been most troublesome. The key is to identify the ways we can alter our holiday experience, by keeping what is rich and meaningful while making an effort to eliminate or alter the sources of the holiday blues.

3. Exercise Imagination

An extension of using creativity is letting holidays become an opportunity to indulge the side of us which goes beyond the humdrum of everyday life. We all understand how so many holidays that involve gifts or cards are imbued with a sense of surprise.   Fortunately, we still have enough of the child's yearning for magic to be delighted in being both the recipient and the provider of surprise. The whole framework of holidays such as Christmas and Hanukah is to let children feel magically delighted by experiences they derive from mythical figures such as Santa Claus, or through the careful generosity of loved ones. We decorate trees, fill our houses with the scents of holiday food, and infuse the period with songs that capture the flavor of celebration.

For those who do not suffer from holiday blues, the need for creativity may not be as great. It is probable that when celebration does not cause pain, that one is able to exercise just enough imagination to be fulfilled by various holidays. There are, however, certain blues patterns that would greatly benefit from an effort to be artful. The Lost Soul, for example, tends to get mired in a downward spiral of self-pity. She often finds herself waiting for an invitation, cards, or general affirmation. A very useful solution for Lost Souls is to work at creating a holiday experience.

When I suggested to a former client that she make herself the center of a holiday such as Thanksgiving, rather than spend another year resenting her "lousy" family and being certain that no invitation would arrive. Her response was predictable. "Everyone I know has family or friends, and would clearly not be available, " she claimed. After much urging and cajoling, she finally agreed to contact an international organization of foreign exchange students who were largely without plans for Thanksgiving. To her surprise, a coordinator of the organization was delighted to hear from her, and quickly rounded up almost a dozen students, including two spouses and their children. After getting over her intense performance anxieties, she was able to host her first Thanksgiving. She told me the experience was incredibly rewarding. She said her guests were not judgmental but simply grateful, and best of all, they had no historical experiences with which to compare her meal.

Another way to exercise creativity is to consider a different setting for celebration. While most families loathe going off to a novel setting, a change of scenery often works wonders. Though some nonobservant Christians, as well as non-Christians, manage to use the winter holidays as an excuse to head south, it is difficult for others to give up the hope of a "White Christmas, " or to forego the task of holiday decorating.

One Merrymaker was having a difficult time saying no to all the holiday opportunities , and was unable to put the brakes on his typical seasonal overindulgence. Hearing how a friend had circumvented some holiday problems, this Merrymaker decided to rent a cottage on the Chesapeake Bay for the end of December. Though his wife resisted, they managed to have a very family-focused holiday without the triggers that usually activated overindulgent behavior. The Merrymaker, his wife, and their two children managed to recapture the feelings they knew were missing from many past seasons.

The same concept of a scenery change also worked wonders for a Perfectionist I know. Leaving for a holiday made it possible to negate all the behaviors associated with ruining the holidays. He and his family decided to travel in Europe, and see how the holidays were observed in Mediterranean countries. They set up an itinerary that included parts of France, Italy, and Spain. While the trip was not intended to have a religious focus, the whole family was so moved by the "cathedral experience" in Italy that they returned with an un-expected newfound affirmation of their faith. Despite a few setbacks, the Perfectionist claimed to have had his best Christmas ever. At the beginning of the trip, his anxious tendencies kicked in, and were directed at the details of the trip. After some intense arguments about who was in charge of planning, he agreed to give up control of the schedule to his willing wife. Once he was comfortable with not having control, his anxiety abated and the holiday started to be fun.

Creativity goes beyond the choice of setting for a celebration. One of the best Father's Day presents ever received from two children was a coupon book redeemable over the next year. The coupons ranged from labor items such as a car wash to the promise of a few breakfasts in bed. A few blank coupons permitted asking them to participate in activities they knew were favored. This particular father actually recalled using unredeemed coupons from what must have been a Father's Day gift of five years ago.

The giving of gifts can be focused on memorable experiences rather than on purchased items. It is not necessary to travel to Europe or other exotic places to make holidays special. A young man recalled that his favorite birthday party was a winter picnic. His mother, father, and sister hiked into the woods with seven nine-year-old boys and managed to cook hot dogs over a small campfire.

4. Be Pro-active; Implement Change

A universal factor for so many blues profiles is the tendency to let troublesome holidays sneak up. Each year, after surviving another negative experience, people tend to heave a deep sigh of relief until all of a sudden, the next holiday draws near once again. There is no fixed law stating that the same experience must be repeated year after year. Nevertheless, if we are to make a serious dent in these problematic tendencies, planning ahead is crucial. As with so many other behavioral problems, implementing a planning process is easier said than done.

Ironically, people become attached to their self-defeating behavior patterns, which is why the change process is not simple. Certainly, in the process of psychotherapy, individuals speak about change only to find that they "forget" or lose the motivation to follow through. It is a revelation to discover how clients fail to maintain a consistent focus on what they are trying to achieve. In professional terms, the process of subverting one's own treatment goals has been referred to as "resistance." We want to overcome problems and function at a higher level, but manage to throw up all kinds of psychological barriers to achieving the changes we seek. This inconsistency is particularly evident in the weight management field, where one sees the most ambitious plans evaporate under the influence of maneuvers we make to keep things the same

Our reasons for resisting change are quite complex, with each psychological model affording its own explanation. Psychoanalytic theories organize the treatment process around helping clients understand and overcome their unconscious resistant tendencies. Behavioral theories focus more on the strength of habit, and the need for repetition in overcoming long-standing problem behaviors. Whatever the theory, we can all agree that change is fraught with barriers that are mostly self-constructed. It is beyond the scope of this book to further explore why we cling to self-defeating patterns.

Making a change to stop smoking, overeating, or engaging in behavior such as that of the Juggler, requires a serious level of commitment coupled with a serious pro-active program.

The Juggler, in particular, needs to make a plan if she is to get through a holiday without the usual chaos. Since waiting until the last minute is the hallmark of this busy individual, she must decide to create a documented, organized flowchart tied to the calendar. Explicit goals need to be met at different points, in advance of the celebration. It is never too soon to begin working on a holiday plan if it means that a serious modification will be possible. It might seem ridiculous, but a woman who was an extreme Juggler made the decision to implement a Christmas plan during the previous summer. Friends and family teased her when she began to make lists and actually shop for gifts months ahead of time. With some encouragement, she persisted, so that by mid-fall she had completed most of her holiday shopping. Interestingly, as Christmas approached, anxiety set in, and she was strongly tempted to revert to her juggling ways. It was not that she needed to get out and enter a frenzy of purchasing; rather, her association to December tempted her to slip back into Juggler mode.

For this particular woman, and for most Jugglers, planning involves much more than the acquisition of presents. It includes making a variety of decisions that can, and usually do, set off spirals of anxiety. Deciding where to spend a holiday and who will be part of the celebration can be crucial. Married couples often have difficulty managing two different extended families, and holiday locations can change from year to year. In addition, the complexity of reconstituted families, where children from different marriages are involved, can create a logistical nightmare. Thus, critical decisions about location and guests should be part of goal setting, and need to be in place before pre-holiday anxiety becomes activated.

The Loner can also benefit greatly by being pro-active. He needs to confront the major holidays all at once and make some decisions by scanning the calendar at the beginning of the year and marking special occasion that are priorities. It is helpful to think of this as a sort of business plan, a document which is familiar to many people. Though there are sad cases of individuals who are truly bereft of social resources, most people reading this book have a much broader social network, including family, than they consider. The Loner is frequently caught off-guard by holidays that are simply experienced as interruptions in the normal flow of time. Thus, as important days are marked on the calendar, people and possible places should also be noted. Deadline dates should be assigned, to help create a cluster of possible connections for each holiday.

Loners often claim that imposing oneself on others' holiday celebrations is easier said than done. What many do not realize is that people with whom they have varying degrees of connections often assume that the Loners' holidays are "covered." This is especially true for divorced people, who always feel they have been excluded as soon as their marriage dissolves. But their friends, and even relatives, have simply not been accustomed to including these individuals in their holiday celebrations. Many Loners frequently put on a "proud face," suggesting that their lives are just fine, rather than being truthful. It is difficult to be honest, for it can be embarrassing to admit you have no plans for a particular holiday. Nevertheless, when Loners are candid about their situation, it is usually heartening to find that there are many people willing to open their experiences to others in need.

Let's be realistic, though: it may turn out that there is no suitable way to spend a particular holiday with significant acquaintances. Fortunately, many other individuals in our society are in the same boat. Planning a ski trip, ranch vacation, or a holiday cruise with a social emphasis can make a person forget about being alone. What's important is that those who are sufficiently pro-active can stay ahead of the process and not get caught off-guard. If no plan is possible, then any of us can simply accept that we will and can be alone, and choose some fulfilling way to spend the found time of a holiday.

5. Adjust Expectations

So many individuals who suffer from the holiday blues experience a letdown after the holiday ends. This phenomenon of disappointment can range from a brief period of sadness to a significant depression. Indeed, psychotherapists often have numerous new referrals in January, which can also be a period of grieving for their current client group. It does not matter what the occasion. This grief reaction may follow a birthday or a religious holiday, but seems to be most pervasive after Christmas and Hanukah.

The Fixer is especially likely to experience disappointment. This individual, you may recall, approaches holiday gatherings with a determination that this year will be different, better than the year before. Whether the problem has to do with religious observance, familial participation, or even self-criticism, there is pressure for things to turn out in a better way. Probably the most common theme concerns the behavior of other family members. Poor table manners, lack of reverence, or typical dysfunctional family dynamics are often the target. Perhaps there is an aggressor, a withdrawn family member, or someone who tells the same bad jokes every year. A high level of tension may not be easy to identify, and might be even more difficult to fix.

There are two reasons the Fixer usually ends up feeling blue. One is that he rarely manages to find the right moment or way to have an impact on the situation. Family gatherings have a momentum and consistency, which are often a strong reflection of the personalities involved. Furthermore, just as individuals resist change, so do families. They behave in problematic ways for many reasons and cannot or will not change on command. The Fixer may be accused of being a "spoil sport" if he confronts others, and is often pushed into acceptance by a group process. The second reason is that often, the ambitious Fixer does not really do what he intends, so the sarcastic sister-in-law continues her caustic comments, or his father continues to insult his mother's holiday preparation, year after year.

It is possible that in some families, a good dialogue at the right time will really improve a situation. The whole premise of applied psychology is that change can occur through timely intervention, either by family members and friends or by a professional. However, change generally requires either an openness on the part of others or the willingness of the Fixer to alter the situation by taking a dramatic stand. Sometimes a well-placed piece of "theater," such as boycotting an event or staging a walkout, can leave its mark on others. Sometimes enlisting another family member to join forces in one's noble remedial cause can achieve results.

However, the Fixers who end up with holiday blues are usually unsuccessful. Often, they just stew over what they see

with a feeling of failure and disappointment. Most importantly, they have not made the determination that they probably
cannot and maybe should not tamper with a situation that
will continue to frustrate them. Paradoxically, when Fixers decide to relax their hopes for a different outcome, they actually have a better experience. Sometimes, in this more relaxed
state, it is possible to make a few small changes, which can
certainly add up over the years.

There are other individuals who are constantly let
down by celebrations. They get the "that's all there is?" feeling over and over. The gifts they received were not quite right,
the party for their birthday had the wrong guests, or the holiday just did not touch them in the right way. These people
need to be reoriented to the meaning of the celebration at
hand. They are often bored or disenchanted with some aspect
of their life, and channel that unhappiness into their holidays. For them, the glass is always half empty. This reaction is
sad for the individual, and often has a very negative effect on
co-celebrants. Nothing feels worse than putting a huge effort
into acknowledging a special event for someone who clearly
acts disappointed or is not enthusiastic.

There is probably no singular explanation for this
chronic lack of satisfaction, but one has to suspect that its origins are rooted deeply in childhood. Though it is tempting to
think of this "nothing quite makes it" reaction as a kind of
"spoiled brat" syndrome, that has not been my experience.
These individuals seem to speak more of deficiency in their
backgrounds. While one would suppose that acts of generosity or immersion in festive moments would be greatly appreciated, something different can happen. Lack of consistent
and straightforward satisfaction can actually disrupt chil-

dren's ability to receive. This is similar to individuals who are never complimented and, therefore, become awkward and even suspicious in the face of affirmation. Oddly enough, sometimes the most attractive individuals are uncomfortable with compliments.

It would be a mistake not to include those people who really were overindulged in their childhood. They indeed have a frame of reference for the sensational, so that anything less can cause disappointment. This group is probably growing larger right now, as it seems to be the dilemma of the modern affluent parents to ask if their children have too much. Given the current popularity for providing children with big events and gifts, it is hard to duplicate these in adulthood. So many older adults I speak to can recall just a few birthday parties in their childhood. Yet if I ask a 25-year-old about his or her birthday celebrations, it is not inconceivable to hear "I had one every year." Children's parties seem to grow more lavish every year, with catered food, live entertainment, and large assemblages of their classmates. For children from an affluent Jewish family, it is possible that nothing in their lives will ever compete with their bar/bat mitzvah.

The pattern of responding with disappointment is not easy to break. It is often a reflexive, emotional response embedded in the personality structure of the individual. The best way to combat it is to sign on for a personal values retraining. This reorientation process often involves learning a new way to seek pleasure, with an emphasis on experience rather than material things. Moving celebrations into more natural settings is one of the keys. For example, a "spoiled" woman enrolled in an Outward Bound-type experience on a sailboat. She proudly announced upon her return that learning to "relieve herself" over the side of the boat in front of a group of strangers was the beginning of her new outlook on life. She was not kidding, for she had really developed an appreciation for life's more substantive activities. With the help of family and friends, she was able to call a moratorium on being given anything at all.

6. Be Present

The ability to be fully attuned to the present is not only at the heart of celebration, but is a crucial element of a fulfilling life. However, this experience of being centered in the present, and able to participate in the situation at hand, is not as easy as it might sound. We all live complex lives where we are deal with the residue of what *just* happened, or we are beginning to look past our current experiences in anticipation of what we have to do next or, perhaps, want to do next. Our temporal rhythm becomes disturbed by the pace of modern society. As technology has developed our ability to live with smaller and smaller time units, our capacity to be tyrannized by time has grown proportionately. It is a great paradox that while we have a dazzling array of time savers embedded in our lives, the scarcest commodity is time itself.

At the end of the 20th century, we witnessed an explosion in human convenience technology. Our household labor has been alleviated by dishwashers, vacuum cleaners, washers/dryers, self-cleaning ovens, and a new concept in maintenance called the condominium association. Our communication process has been revolutionized by fax machines, beepers, television, e-mail, overnight mail to distant sites, cell phones, and on the near horizon—video telephones. We use drive-throughs for food and banking, and will soon be doing most our shopping online. Yet despite all the capacity for time saving, we are, in a sense, at war with time. Think of that universal refrain: "I don't have the time."

As a result of shortening time intervals, we have completely changed our pace so that rather than acquiring time, we are trying to function in sync with the devices we have invented. The frantic pace we keep obviously makes it very difficult to pause for a holiday. Our attention is divided, and we do not allow ourselves time and space for a proper celebration. *Ironically, the more crowded our lives become with plans and activities, the more we need genuine holidays to refresh us.* The real question, of course, is how to break with the frantic pace and be present for a holiday. In a sense, many of us are Jugglers who function in a time compression, running from one part of our lives to another.

Being present involves two components. First, we must intentionally shut out all the interferences that are under our control. We must allow enough time for the holiday to have meaning, rather than celebrating it "on the fly." Do not, for example, try to celebrate someone's birthday while there are other pressures impinging on the celebration. It would be better to delay the occasion (if the birthday is for an adult) rather than make someone feel that her special day was a burden. Try to eliminate the intrusions that detract from focusing on the here and now. Many of these intruders are relatively new to our lives, although some are all too familiar. Television has competed with the quality of holidays for several decades, and should probably be turned off by decree of those in charge. Granted, some families derive great satisfaction from

Thanksgiving football or New Year's Day bowl games. It is certainly acceptable, so long as the television is being viewed by consensus and no rift is caused by watching the games.

The telephone has been an annoyance for at least 50 years and needs to be managed. Teenagers, in particular, need to suspend their connections to their social world for the few hours that all holidays require. While teenagers can be the most obvious in their disconnection from the event, beepers and cellular phones are the enemy for everyone at the social gathering. All these conveniences should be put on hold while the focus shifts to religious observance or the acknowledgment of a special day. Yes, even the physicians, lawyers, psychologists, and others who are electronically linked must make the effort to turn off their gadgets.

The computer, our newest competitor for attention, must also be contained during holiday time. E-mail and on-line dialogue can be postponed for a while. Attachment to the Internet has replaced television addiction in some families. The "need" to be online in dialogues, games, or surfing has become a divisive family issue for both daily life as well as for holidays. Though it may not be practical or feasible for everyone to go away somewhere on a holiday, there can be tremendous merit in separating from all the detractors. It really does not matter where the celebration occurs. If the laptop, cell phone, and portable fax are left behind, there is a greater chance to be immersed in the present with family or friends. The transition away from our solitary gadgets in not always easy. Families who have gotten accustomed to not being present without distraction have to relearn, or even acquire, the ability to simply be together.

The second component of being present is more difficult than making rules about the intrusion of modern technology. Regulating one's focus to fully engage in the immediate present is easier said than done. It takes discipline to shut out the past, and avoid drifting into thoughts about the near or distant future. This problem of staying centered in the present comes up all the time for parents of young children. A working mother started psychotherapy specifically because she was not able to fully immerse herself in the interests and activities of her preschool-age daughter after a "grueling day" in her software business. "No matter how I tried," she complained, "after a few minutes of reading or talking about her concerns, my mind would drift to dinner, household tasks, or business." This client is obviously not alone in her inability to fully invest in the here and now. The solution for this working mother was twofold. First, she had to reassess the time interval devoted to her daughter. Second, she had to really work to defocus other considerations through some sustained training in thought regulation. Adult attention problems have recently been the focus of both research and clinical work. It has been difficult to fully ascertain whether we are dealing with some newly classified biochemical phenomenon or a broad-scale reaction to the rhythm of our lifestyles.

Holidays are a perfect framework for change in the continuity of our lives. They force us to break away from routine and to focus on the celebration at hand. Most religions have a weekly Sabbath structure, intended to push us into a reflective state. Observant individuals of all faiths often welcome the chance to pause and immerse themselves in a present-centered experience through prayer or other routine. For those who are not observant, the quest for focus on the present may be sought through meditation, spending time outdoors, or immersion in hobbies. There are no sure-fire or quick solutions to the need for being present. One of the compelling aspects of human sexuality is the opportunity to be a full participant in the here-and-now with one's partner.

As with a Sabbath experience, holidays should be approached as opportunities for a refreshing break. There should be self-awareness about the flow of consciousness, as when one is trying to pay attention to the conversation of a child. The ability to change the habit of being distracted requires work and commitment. Start by observing your conversation with a person close to you. Focus on making sure that person is fully heard, and that your responses are truly related to his or her thoughts and feelings. To be truly empathic, the response must reflect the content of the dialogue. Too often, we find people adrift in their own concerns, so that conversation seems to be parallel rather than interactive. If we can master the art of meaningful dialogue, the same can be done for being present. The task is to observe the *time frame* of our thought patterns as a holiday experience is occurring. Work on interrupting thoughts that drift into the past or future. As this temporal "tuning" proceeds, the capacity for real holiday fulfillment will increase dramatically.

This process of self-monitoring is crucial for certain holiday blues profiles. The Mourner, for example, has an especially difficult time being fully present, given an automatic longing for the celebration of holidays during some other period of life. Often, the memories that interfere with present celebrations come from either the real or imagined past. Remember that negative experiences are recalled in different forms, and in many cases, are idealized. These recollections of a "perfect" past make the current event disappointing, resulting in sadness. Of course, sometimes the feelings associated with the past are simply terrific and cannot be duplicated. That's fine, but it does not help anyone celebrate in an upbeat way. More than any other blues profile, the Mourner really has to divest him/herself of these memories. If the sadness does not represent a repudiation of one's current life situation, there is a very useful way to stop making these destructive comparisons. Rather than see the present holiday in terms of a historical recollection, reinvent it. The best way is to change the place and style in a radical way. I previously mentioned the possibilities inherent in traveling to a foreign location. Sometimes it is necessary to go so far as to take a year off from holiday celebrations, in an attempt to break connections. Remember, holidays are to be anticipated as pauses. If they are triggers for sadness or anxiety, something should change.

7. Practice Altruism

During the holidays, try extending your generosity and energies to others. Not only is putting thought into the care and well-being of others consistent with our cultural values, but the act of giving seems to have inherent value for any individual. *There is no better antidote for the self-absorption associated with holiday blues than to get outside yourself and consider the plight of other individuals.* Most dictionaries define altruism as a selfless action, which is obviously at the other end of the spectrum from the emotional states such as anger and frustration that characterize many people's holiday experience.

Older people who reach a point of economic security, or who find that circumstances have necessitated a withdrawal from their business or jobs, must come up with a retirement plan. That is not to say that everyone is exactly successful at pre-retirement planning. Some individuals simply cannot wait to live with what they view as an absence of goal setting. Others sense that retirement without structure is a hazardous affair, and try to engineer a life that is meaningful. Inevitably, a large percentage of retired people put volunteer work at the center of their schedules. There may be travel or part-time work, but altruistic inclinations figure in the plans of many.

To young people or even busy middle-aged individuals, volunteering might seem like a way to stay busy or keep out of trouble. Upon further examination, it is far more profound than a simple way to pass time. There is something redeeming and deeply satisfying about helping a person, a group, or an institution without economic compensation. For many people, it provides a contrast with what they have accomplished, as well as a way to give back something of *themselves*. A good example is a client who owned a successful printing company for many years. He described the last decade before he sold his business as "sheer drudgery." He was tired of the mean-spirited, bottom-line approach to dealing with both his customers and his employees. He had always wished he were in a profession where he helped people, and saw his retirement as an opportunity to shift gears. He decided to become an advocate for foster children who were having serious trouble with their placements. To be fully informed, he actually took a six-month course in child welfare law. He claimed that this work fully dominated his life, and that he could not wait for each workday to begin.

The desire to perform service is certainly not limited to retired people. Women who are not in the workplace have traditionally been involved in cultural and civic institutions, providing an invaluable economic and labor asset. Young people can also derive tremendous fulfillment from making volunteerism a part of their lives. Especially during the highly self-centered years of high school and college, this work can be an essential element in maintaining balance. It is simply more difficult to overindulge in the excesses of adolescence while also doing something like volunteering at a children's hospital. Extending oneself to a sick child or a new immigrant creates a sense of self-worth and perspective that is so hard to attain.

It is not accidental that in discussing altruism the focus, ironically, has been on what generosity can do for the giver. It goes without saying that service to others has immutable social value. Every religion of the world has emphasized charity as a central part of its ideals. All of our holidays, especially Christmas and Hanukah, are infused with the concept of sharing our wealth. Schools and religious institutions constantly emphasize the importance of contributing to worthwhile causes, especially by giving to the less advantaged. Children bring packaged foods to school, and many people put something in the Salvation Army kettle. For the most part, however, altruism is an afterthought for the majority of us, especially around holidays when our emphasis in on the pressing demands of the "production."

Donating money is certainly one way to be altruistic, and is necessary for the maintenance of programs and institutions. But money can and should be dispersed throughout the year as budgets permit and as needs arise both domestically and internationally. It is always terrific to see how the western world, especially the United States, mobilizes relief efforts in response to both natural and man-made calamity. There is, however, a commodity we can share which is perhaps more sacred to us than our financial assets–namely, *time*. Giving up familiar routines and activities in the service of a cause requires deep and more meaningful commitment. Watching people mobilize after a devastating hurricane to assemble and ship vital supplies, or to actually travel to the afflicted region, is inspiring to everyone. Many of us marvel at these efforts, but it seems that only a few have the wherewithal, generosity, and courage to actually take the time.

It is easy to give time around the holidays since it is possible to plan how and when to donate. There is no question that it feels right, and gives anyone inclined to altruism a greater sense of celebration. The question is how people can act on their urges to do more than simply indulge in the excesses of parties, feasts, and gift-giving orgies.

Paul established a tradition for himself and his family many years ago. When he was beginning to prosper in business, he and his son would buy a shopping cart full of toys for an orphanage every Christmas. As a family, they would wrap the presents, which would be delivered to the orphanage each year anonymously, without fanfare. Each year the ritual expanded, to the point that it seems to require an entire day to shop and wrap the presents, which have become an important part of the orphanage's Christmas celebration.

A young couple was complaining that they had become caricatures of "yuppies." They felt that their busy careers and recreational habits had fostered a kind of self-absorption that was contradictory to their values. Both had volunteered in high school and wanted to recapture that experience as a couple. They thought their relationship had become bogged down in business dialogues and a repugnant materialism, so they decided to change their usual Thanksgiving plans and spend the day helping to prepare and serve dinner in a homeless shelter. Essentially, they canceled their own plans for dinner with their astonished families to spend the better part of Thanksgiving with people they would normally shun on a crowded city street. The result was, somehow, not surprising. The couple was elated, and said it was probably their most meaningful holiday. Not only did altruism give them a profound sense of satisfaction, but they found the chance to meet and understand the people at the shelter to be "amazing." They developed an ongoing relationship with a single mother and her teenage son. Additionally, they are planning to take a more active part in the shelter, but emphasize that they do not intend to give up the role they played on a significant holiday.

Many of us say that we cannot do anything like this young couple because we have children or other critical obligations. Children, however, are not always thrilled with our celebrations, and respond better than adults when given the opportunity to extend themselves. The nature of so many charitable projects allows children to work alongside older siblings, friends, and, most important, parents. Children rarely get the opportunity to function in a competent way, and to be part of meaningful work. While children in less developed parts of the world, especially in rural areas, are expected to participate in the business of life, our affluent offspring mostly play at life. They do not get the chance to tend livestock or partake in the construction or maintenance of family dwellings. Many contemporary parents have a difficult time getting their children to do more than grudgingly perform token household chores. However, when given the opportunity to get involved with community reclamation projects, they simply love it. A young teenage boy achieved national celebrity status by spearheading a program to distribute bedding to homeless people during his winter holiday. A few years ago when President Clinton assembled a formidable cast of prominent individuals to clean up a part of Philadelphia, the response of children was inspiring.

It is really our own inhibition and, in a sense, laziness, that keeps us from doing what we say we want to do on holidays. So many of us recognize that self-absorption is contradictory to our religious and personal values, that our holidays suffer from an absence of substance, and that they are in need of creative revision. Sometimes our self-image keeps us from generosity because of fears that we will be seen as "corny do-gooders," and so we allow the altruistic urges to fall to other people, or we tuck them away for the proverbial "next year." As with all the recommendations for dealing with the holiday blues, it's best to start small and operate within the scope of what is consistent with the view of ourselves. By taking these realistic steps, paradoxically, the opportunity to see ourselves differently becomes possible.

8. Focus on Relationships

Most holidays are meant to occur for or with significant others. Every Thanksgiving and Christmas the roads are filled with pilgrims traveling to celebrate with others, often family. The pull to be social is so strong that, even when people speak of the dreadful time they have every year, they keep going back for more! In our mobile society with so many transplanted individuals, certain holidays become a "no brainer" when it comes to family. Grudges and wounds, fresh and old, get put on hold as people assemble to acknowledge special days.

It is difficult to think of celebration in the absence of social context. Though social networks have certainly weakened, certain events simply do not seem the same without a group. Though I have not specifically mentioned them, wedding and funerals are occasions that illustrate the importance of other people. It is always enlightening to see how long-lost relatives manage to turn up when there is a family wedding. Funerals, also, have a power to evoke the participation of the extended family. It is as if we all acknowledge that certain events in the life cycle simply take precedence over accumulated grudges.

These obligatory assemblages have a restorative quality, in that they can alter the course of relationships that have stopped being viable. Imperfect seating plans at weddings force estranged family members to eat, drink, and celebrate together. Perhaps images from childhood are evoked, and defenses are dropped long enough for relationships to be rekindled. One of the most salient discoveries from my research in East Africa was directly related to this healing power of the family assemblage. Based on spending many hours in observation of and conversation with some very prominent shamen, their approach to treating certain forms of anxiety and depression was remarkable. Often, they would refer their urban patients back to their tribal homes to partake in a feast involving large extended families. They had to sleep in their traditional homes and forego Western dress, paraphernalia, and status for several days. After some days of reconnecting with their families of origin, the reasoning was that balance would be restored to these individuals. This "treatment" is not unlike the possibilities inherent in every family gathering. It would be wonderful if they all had such happy endings.

We may not always find ourselves in a position to be connected to others on special days. Job relocations, divorces, and military assignments all take us away from our usual social network. Even without these special circumstances, there are individuals who simply find themselves without people with whom to celebrate. Many complicated personalities, such as Loners, may not have been able to acquire or sustain friendships. They may be estranged from their families, or have never developed the kind of friendships that are helpful around holidays. Big cities are filled with such individuals who coexist with many people, but without significant connections. Their celebrations can occur in a solitary way as they take the time that holidays create to seek some special experience. I have generally found, however, that it is better to coax Loners into some social context even when the relationships are not very deep. Ironically, since we know that family gatherings are not always precious, celebrations with strangers can prove equally or even more satisfying. Spending Thanksgiving at an International House gathering of students or visitors is usually far more satisfying than trying to construct a self-satisfying experience. Though many Loners may extol the holiday experience they had alone, there is often a sense that solitary celebration is second best.

The components of a holiday should never take precedence over the well-being of the people who partake in it. There are many ways this rule should apply, and it is relevant to just about every blues profile. If we begin with the notion of the celebration as a mini-production, the success of that production should be measured by the satisfaction of the guests. So often with the Perfectionist or the Juggler, the emphasis is entirely on "getting it right." The meal, the decorations, the timing, or the presents become the focus. It is inevitable that things will not, and probably should not, go perfectly. Even Broadway productions vary from night to night only to the awareness of the actors and directors. A dish on the menu may be over-cooked or forgotten, the decorations imperfect, and the re-sponse to gifts will necessarily be variable. We often think it is the receiver of generosity who must be grateful and not show poor manners by grimacing in the face of a disappointing pre-sent. The same should be said of the giver's response to the way his/her effort is appreciated.

A recently married woman had been given an anniver-sary necklace by her husband. He was extremely proud of his present and spoke at length about how he had searched high and low for just the right piece of jewelry which, he reminded her, was the most expensive gift he had ever purchased. As you might guess, she did not like anything about the necklace, feel-ing that it was not her taste and that she would actually be em-barrassed to wear it. Her dilemma was that her "sensitive" hus-band would be devastated to learn her true feelings. Obviously, their relationship suffered from some serious communication inhibitions. She needed to find a gentle way to be relieved of the burden to wear something she found so uncomfortable.

This situation of the fragile giver happens over and over, during all the occasions we celebrate. People plan sur-prise parties, buy exotic gifts, and put tremendous energy into doing something impressive for others. Unfortunately, all too frequently, it is the giver who is looking for accolades, which do not always come. It is not uncommon for hard feelings or even fights to occur when the receiver does not show just the right amount of enthusiasm. The same disappointment may arise when guests at a holiday party seem indifferent or unresponsive to the efforts put forth by their host.

The key to making holidays successful is to understand and, as much as possible, accept the taste and needs of other people. A perfect production is not successful if the audience is not appreciative and wants to leave by intermission. The same can said about elaborate preparations for holiday meals. Conflicts arise regarding demeanor, pace and about manner of dress. We live in a very casual, fast-paced culture where children and some adults cannot or will not tolerate formality. Such matters of taste and style need to be diplomatically discussed in advance, rather than causing wounds when one branch of the family shows up for a formal Thanksgiving dinner wearing warm-up suits or jeans. On the other hand, though people are always griping about having to dress up, at the same time there is a sense of real satisfaction when dressing for a special occasion. That's why black-tie New Year's parties are so popular—formal attire seems to have the capacity to set the occasion apart, as holidays are intended to do.

More important than gifts and decorum is the potential that exists for making contact with people. If the celebration is an anniversary or birthday, be sure not only to honor the recipient with appropriate cards and gifts, but also to really focus on the person. While there is nothing wrong with store-bought greeting cards, there is something especially moving about a personal note that addresses the meaning of the occasion. Though some think that the family updates commonly mailed at Christmas are corny, they at least get past the impersonal "Season's Greetings" message and convey what the sender deems important. Relationships are one of the most valuable resources, and one of the best ways to maintain them is by keeping significant people in your life informed

It is not a bad idea to see a holiday gathering as a chance to deepen relational bonds. Improving on existing relationships becomes possible when people gather and attempt to open themselves to the experience of others. It is amazing how often we spend time with family only to find that the same conversation seems to take place year after year. One can leave a gathering realizing that no meaningful information was transmitted, and that few personal questions were asked. It is very worthwhile to set some conversational goals before a holiday gathering. Decide to make inquiries about some new family member or resolve not to participate in some spiteful joking about a particular person. The point is not to get caught in the "Fixer," trap where expectations become unrealistic and frustrating. Try to push the group into more dialogue by relying less on activities such as games. People who have not seen each other for long periods of time should probably not retreat to card games, word games, or sports as a way to relate. All of these activities are fine, but not as a substitute for real dialogue.

Something as simple as creating a tradition of a family walk can force people into conversation. One of the striking differences between holidays in the United States and in Europe has to do with post-meal behavior. When I visited Bologna, Italy a few years ago, I was astonished to see that the streets were filled with people on Christmas Day, just strolling in conversation while searching for familiar faces to join them. Though our highways are overloaded on holidays, our streets are strikingly empty. Taking a walk is simple; it slows everything down, facilitating both the digestion of the feast and the conversation which is the foundation of all relationships.

9. Have Patience

We live in a society where we expect things to happen and change in an instant. The concept of the "quick fix" is endemic to our way of life. One can look to our obsession with weight loss and body image. Books, magazine articles, and television advertising, as well as pharmaceutical and holistic diet products, all testify to the enormity of our preoccupation with weight. Countless individuals yield to the temptation to use diet pills when other approaches fail to work. The results are pretty much the same every time: short-term weight loss followed by a gradual return to the prior weight. In some cases, people actually gain more weight than they originally carried before starting the pills. This last point is the most relevant in our discussion of making changes for the holidays. Pills tend to make us passive as we wait for the chemicals to suppress our appetite or speed up our metabolism. Rather than working on the attitudes and habits that contribute to the weight problem, there is a drop-off in our willingness to work. In order to achieve lasting changes, we must remain focused, disciplined, perseverant, and, above all, patient.

It is difficult to change behavior, especially when it is rooted in our personalities as well as our personal and family histories. Jugglers notably approach many aspects of their lives with the same intensity and potential disorganization. Merrymakers are likely to overindulge, in general, and take their habits to extremes. Lost Souls tend to be lost in self-pity for much of their lives, and during the holidays this experience simply deepens. The point is that we have tendencies in the directions of our blues patterns which, in a sense, represent part of ourselves and our identities. When looking to break a long-standing pattern, it is important not to become discouraged after a brief, abortive effort. *It is important to think of celebration as a piece of art that can be worked and reworked until it represents the image we desire.*

In a way, successfully dealing with holiday blues patterns is much like psychotherapy itself. Clients, as well as observers, often ask why the process takes so long and why so many individuals remain in therapy, sometimes for years. Though the answer might be different depending upon the particular school of psychotherapy, in general, all psychologists will agree that change takes repetition and practice. It is fairly easy to make a diagnostic assessment, but it is not as easy to bring about enduring change. Though there are isolated quick changes, epiphanies if you will, for the most part change occurs with two steps forward and one step back. Unfortunately, sometimes the two steps are backward instead, so that progress is not necessarily linear. The process of growth and change is often marked by an ambivalence which psychoanalytic clinicians have termed *resistance*. The concept of resistance suggests that all of us have mixed feelings about change. Doing things differently or even experiencing them from a fresh perspective disturbs our equilibrium, drawing us back to what is familiar.

Joan, a 42-year-old homemaker, had established the tradition of having her family and her husband's family over to celebrate the Easter Sunday. All of her Perfectionist tendencies were channeled into the meal which, because of her elaborate menu, lent itself to tremendous detail. She came to see me for broader reasons, but in the spring could not avoid talking about her frustration and rage after the holiday was over. She felt that everyone, including her husband, was irreverent, too casual in all respects, and did little to appreciate the work that went into her complex combination of food preparation and its presentation. She felt as though the whole group, including her husband and children, were "conspiring" to undermine her effort to create a beautiful holiday experience.

Joan had a difficult time translating the work we did in therapy to her blues patterns. The first year that she attempted to focus more on the meaning of the holiday and to try to relate to her family members without the residual irritation, her plan backfired. She perceived that as she withdrew her "controls," things deteriorated, proving that it was she who had to control the quality of the experience for everyone else.

Joan was not exercising patience with the change process. In fairness to all blues sufferers, it is difficult to be patient when the investment in a celebration is high and such an occasion comes only once a year. Changing holiday dynamics is not like changing eating habits, where the opportunity for confronting undesirable behavior occurs on a daily basis. One's perspective must be broadened so that each holiday is perceived as a piece of the larger fabric of life, rather than an all-or-nothing event. After Joan's first "failure," she said something like, "By the time things are the way I want them, my children will already be grown." She had to understand that if she were really concerned about the quality of her children's Easter, she would do better to *gradually* make the desired changes and expunge the anger from her religious observance.

10. Help!

Holiday blues patterns tend to go on year after year despite the loudest proclamations that next year will be different. "I will never invite those people again," or, "Next year, we're putting a budget on what we spend," are heard over and over again. As I have discussed, these patterns are deeply entrenched in our sense of self and also tend to be continuously reinforced by our social contexts. We all live in interpersonal or social systems that can "enable" us in our self-defeating patterns of behavior. Even if the others in our social world do not reinforce the wrong behavior, they serve as reminders or cues to behave in a certain way.

Looking at Joan and her Easter problem, it is clear that she needed to enlist her family and guests before she could be successful in making the adjustments she desired. Since the source of so many holiday problems concerns our connections to other people, it makes a great deal of sense to seek out their support, understanding, and encouragement. In a case like Joan's, there are two ways for her to get some help from her family. First, considering her perfectionism, she might let them know she was going to try to loosen her controlling grip on the event. In explaining this, she would need to ask that they be aware of her plan, to avoid letting things slip further and, more importantly, so that they did not tease or joke about the change. A second way in which they might help is that Joan could ask them to join forces and pick up her perfectionism where she leaves off. This is easier said than done, since a Perfectionist does not easily hand over control. Moreover, there is likely to be some resistance if people pay lip service to the plan. There will certainly be a participant or two who have always resented Joan's rigidity and might not be so thrilled to assume her posture.

Another example of the need for family help can be seen in the case of a Merrymaker, who resolves every New Year's not to go so far into debt with Christmas expenditures. Somehow, though the desire is authentic enough, each December the plan is adhered to briefly and then scrapped as forces come into play. The first force has to do with how alien the concept is to the merrymaker who has trouble conceiving of the holidays without a big economic splash. The other forces come from immediate and extended family. It is difficult, in particular, to draw children into an austerity program as they are bathed in a sea of commercialism and high material expectation. Explaining why, all of a sudden, Dad or Mom is on some "new kick," sure to ruin the holidays, takes a great deal of concerted, consistent effort. For the single parent, it is even more difficult to have to play the bad guy, especially if there is a divorced parent who will continue the lavish spending. Children, however, can be persuaded, for they are still malleable and will ultimately accept the family's values. More often than not, the reticence to cut back lays with the overindulger, not with the kids.

Large extended families can also make it difficult to implement a change of venue. A single young man from a small town in rural Maryland had seven siblings, all of whom were married, had children, and loved to exchange at least three presents each. One year he recalled wrapping more than 60 presents, about which he had little excitement and for which he went into debt as usual. His initial pleas to cut back, first to his parents and then to his siblings, were rejected. He went through a great deal of pain and perceived rejection when he tried to downscale the scope of the purchasing. Success did not come until he was able to convince one brother and one sister, who were not financially flourishing themselves, that a "Pollyanna" would be much better for everyone. Though the children resisted his idea, he reported that after a few years they actually began toasting him as a hero at every Christmas dinner!

There are times when it simply pays to seek professional help to expedite the process of change. It is not typical for individuals to start psychotherapy simply to work on their perceived blues pattern. Most people do not necessarily realize that they have the holiday blues. What typically happens is that they react to an impending celebration or find themselves depressed in the wake of a holiday. The majority of blues patterns, most evident around Christmas, anniversaries, birthdays, and Mother's and Father's Day, all have the same evocative power. Typically, most psychologists become very busy in the aftermath of Christmas and New Year's—if one doesn't get you, then the other will! It is not always clear to the individual that there is a holiday connection, but it does not take long to establish the relationship. When a holiday disappointment triggers a major depression, the individual tends to seek help for the depression. When depression is at its worst, it is not easy to have insight into its origins or causes. Thought processes become cloudy, and negative feelings overwhelm the ability to reason productively.

It is more common to work on holiday blues problems with patients who are in therapy for other purposes. This situation is, from a professional viewpoint, the optimal way to tackle holiday issues. There is the chance to get to know the client, to assemble a family history, and, as various celebrations begin to approach, there can be anticipatory planning which allows the client to be pro-active. It is a good idea for all practicing clinicians to have an outline of the holidays that are relevant to a particular patient. Though most therapists are conscientious when it comes to medical and psychiatric histories, I have found that they do not typically ascertain holiday data. As a result, it is easy to miss the reactions clients have to upcoming dates, and to miss the opportunity to use the dynamics of celebrations to illuminate the therapy process.

Elsa, a 50-year-old psychotherapy client, was not religious, rather cynical, and really never let on that any holidays had much importance to her. In fact, she seemed neutral about them, and participated in her friends' and families' celebrations without much fanfare. It took a while for me to realize that her mood dropped off during the summer months, which are not typically seen as a holiday season. Further inquiry revealed that she would become upset as Memorial Day approached because of deep-seated concerns about her body image. Always vain, she had described herself as very fit until she turned 40, when she had been married and divorced twice. She brought photos into a therapy session that dramatically illustrated the difference in her appearance between the past and the present. She claimed that she could only wear a bathing suit in "the islands," and even then was very self-conscious. It was easy to be fooled, as the subjects of food, body image, and summer activities never really came up. When asked why it took so long for her to get to this very nuclear issue, she said she was embarrassed and thought that a male therapist probably would not understand. The point here is that a comprehensive job of inquiring about holidays had not been done, and there was insufficient focus on her plans for

Memorial Day or July Fourth when most of her friends would gather at the beach.

It is reasonable to ask whether individuals can solve the problem of celebration by themselves. It is not only possible, but also reasonable, to assume that if a holiday issue is not a manifestation of some broader psychological concern, individuals should be expected to tackle it by themselves. I would not expect patients who have an obsessive-compulsive disorder to combat perfectionism without professional help. By the same token, people with a recent history of depression would probably be seen as Mourners, as a result of the depression. However, short of a diagnosable psychological disorder, it should be possible to make a self-assessment based on the categories highlighted in this book. The evaluation should note both the sensitive holidays and the associated patterns of behavior.

It is very important to realize that the concept of self-help can be somewhat artificial. From childhood on, we are all engaged in a developmental process that involves a great deal of self-generated learning, while we configure how we will live our lives. Certainly there are vast differences in the personal freedoms we exercise. Some people develop an identity associated with their parents, and continue to do things in a rather proscribed way. Others rebel to different degrees, and fashion their own paths in life through trial and error. Wherever one falls on this continuum, the process of self-help is universal, for we are all engaged in a continual process of reflection. This process comes much more easily for some who have developed the ability to stand back and reflect on their lives, unlike others who seem to be on "auto pilot." Reflective individuals are generally more durable, in that they can understand and process novel feelings and situations with greater ease. Ultimately, people are helping themselves as long as they do not remain static in the face of problems. Whether they seek the help of friends, family, or a professional, they are *taking action*, and that is what is important.

Should you attempt to reconstruct your approach to a holiday without seeking outside assistance, let me offer a few suggestions. After a period of self-assessment, it is really a good idea to write out an action plan as to how the problem will be tackled. Try to select from among the commandments above. It is unlikely that one by itself will be sufficient, so I would choose three points of attack on which to focus. The schedule might include: (a) Search for Meaning, (b) Exercise Choice, and (c) Seek Help from a Family Member. The plan needs to be put into very concrete form with dates. This approach is much like a business plan, which incorporates goals and has a critical schedule outlining the important times to accomplish goals. Many individuals have found that a holiday diary can be helpful. Keep notes on a daily basis, indicating downward thoughts and feelings, and being sure to assess the degree to which your plan is moving forward.

A very important element of this process is to be fully honest with yourself. Note your reluctance to actually carry out your "threat" to change, as well as the source of obstacles to that change. It is critical to remember that change evokes resistance from ourselves as well as from others. Identify the roadblocks and make plans for overcoming them. The value of patience cannot be overestimated, since it is always easy to say, "What the heck, I'll try again next year." Stick with your goals and program, and expect setbacks. Anyone recovering from addiction or any other serious negative habit knows that

Guide to the Holiday Blues

BLUES PROFILE	SYMPTOMS	PRIMARY FEELING	REMEDY
Juggler	Anxiety, fatigue	Too much on my plate	Pro-active planning
Perfectionist	Anxiety, irritation	Have to get it right	Try new paradigm
Merrymaker	Anxiety, remorse	Don't know when to stop	Clarify values, altruism
Loner	Sadness, isolation	Where has everybody gone?	Communicate needs
Mourner	Sadness, longing	It's not like the good old days	Become fully present
Lost Soul	Sadness, bitterness	No one cares about me	Defocus self; help others
Fixer	Anger, frustration	This year will be better	Adjust expectations
Grinch	Anger, cynicism	Holidays are a nuisance	Self-examination, generosity

a setback cannot be an excuse for abandoning one's commitment to change. Iris, a successful investment advisor, found it very useful to think of each day, when she was overcoming her problem, as an investment. As the days accumulated into months, she became more and more reluctant to give up her investment of time and energy. She always felt it was within her power, and that she could chose to stay the course. It is now more than a year since she overcame a life-threatening habit. Her determination was truly inspirational. In the context of seeking professional help, it really boiled down to finding a personal formula that would inspire her to triumph by ultimately helping herself.

Beyond Survival: 5
Celebrating Positive and Authentic Holidays

For those who dread a particular holiday, getting through it is usually the associated feeling. But survival is an unfortunate approach. So many people live large chunks of their lives by the survival mentality. Children cannot wait until the school year ends, adolescents cannot wait to turn 18, adults cannot wait for their two-week vacation, and older adults live their life on a countdown to retirement. This psychological ploy of living for the next thing, of sacrificing the present, is what philosophically-oriented psychologists have generally termed inauthentic living. Rather than perceiving our lives as finite and wanting to maximize every situation, the survival mentality seems predicated on the illusion that somehow we can afford to squander our time by getting through one situation after another. Yet when directly confronted, most sensible individuals would not want their eulogy to read, "I survived."

When we dread components of our lives, something is either wrong with the situation (e.g., school) or the way we are approaching it. Holidays, like the rest of life, should be positive markers to anticipate with enthusiasm and optimism. In a sense, holidays are a comfortable, repetitive psychological calendar. They are like the seasons of the year, in that they give us an automatic sense of the future. In fact, there is an inextricable relationship between the seasons and the holidays that occur during them. For Jews, the waning days of summer suggest that the high holy days are around the corner. Christians usually associate the first sign of spring with Easter. When people change climates, moving to Florida or Arizona, one adjustment they must make is developing new associations between seasonal changes and the anticipation of special days.

If holidays present a recurring threshold to the future, they also provide an opportunity to underscore what is important. When we no longer dread a particular celebration, we can examine the personal, familial, cultural, and religious values that characterize our lives. Of course, we do not always want to be in a state of constant examination and reflection. Part of the joy of holidays is the sense of constancy, of knowing what to expect with excitement and anticipation. Obviously, some level of periodic assessment is necessary, especially when holidays become detached from their significance. Making celebration a fulfilling part of life is learning to find the right mix of constancy and change. If everything changes from year to year, the uncertainty is unsettling and leads to anxiety. When little changes from year to year, there is the danger of stagnation, especially for those caught in one or more of the debilitating blues patterns.

Constancy

One of the earliest developmental tasks of childhood is the development of what Piaget called *object constancy*. Before children develop this sense of constancy, they become upset by the appearance and disappearance of their nurturers. We play "peek-a-boo" endlessly to help developing children master the anxiety associated with the coming and going of their parents. Before the development takes place, it is common to see perfectly contented children dissolve into instantaneous panic and tears should their mother or father leave the room without warning. We see this anxiety in bold relief as the routine of bedtime is negotiated. New parents are often befuddled by the delicacy of that situation. They might have to appear and reappear in their children's bedroom to the point of exhaustion. It is not uncommon for new parents to yield to this lack of constancy and simply bring their anxious offspring right to their bed. At least, sleep becomes possible again.

This need for constancy is primary to human existence. Even after young children grasp that their parents will return, there are still many test points throughout childhood. The first babysitter, the first day of nursery school, or the presence of a substitute teacher can seriously upend children. In addition to the constancy of significant people, children tend to thrive on routine. They need to eat, nap, play, and go to sleep in a structured way. When structure is difficult, children do not flourish to the same degree. The rituals around bedtime become very established. Reading, storytelling, and, in some cases, prayer, seem to offer the reassurance they need to voluntarily close their eyes, and have the faith that the world will be the same when they awake the next morning.

Adults also need rituals in their lives. Holidays undoubtedly evolved in ancient civilizations to provide adults with expected periodic rituals tied to their belief systems about both natural and supernatural phenomena. Just like children, adults need contexts in which to express their fears and joys in a ceremonial, predictable way. Whether dealing with the uncertainties of life, the unification of families, gratitude for harvest, or the acknowledgment of a deity, holidays evolved to allow for the structured connection to important events and feelings.

Perhaps the role of constancy in celebration can best be understood if we re-examine the connection of holidays to religious observance. What unifies most religions of the world is the strong role of constancy and repetition. Observance occurs on the same Sabbath days, and weekly or daily observance involves highly repetitious recitation. It is through the application of learned ritual that individuals find a way to connect their faith with their own feelings. The comfort people derive from observance is clearly connected to the predictable structure associated with solemnity. No better example of this function exists than the rites of burial or cremation where a process is expected to happen "automatically." Funeral directors are supposed to provide a seamless vehicle so that mourners can express their grief without worrying about detail.

When Americans travel to other parts of the world, they often marvel at the way tradition is maintained around special dates. In Spain, numerous festival days commemorate the nuances of the Catholic faith. Village life is often organized and devoted to the execution of these extravaganzas. Tribal customs in many parts of Africa and the pre-industrial world mark holidays with colorful and energetic celebrations. In the United States and other western countries, we have a harder time maintaining this type of appealing constancy. Technology, the dispersion of families, and the multiplicity of our populations make rituals difficult to enact. Even our religious institutions often struggle in trying to hold on to the core of their faith while also appeasing the increasing secular tastes of our culture.

Our capacity for change and self-examination is not necessarily a bad thing. Western civilization derives its vitality from an ability to evolve and accommodate new people and ideas. The problem is how to provide life with a sense of constancy in the context of continuous movement. The answer to this problem is probably twofold. We saw, in looking at the specific holiday blues profiles, that the absence of clear values led to difficulties in celebrating. When values are considered and clarified, it becomes much easier to establish priorities. So many of us have grown up with such an extreme sense of relativity that we find it hard to declare certain days and practices as absolute. Unsure of our identities, we search for new and better ways of celebrating the holidays we value. It is extremely important to continuously solidify our identity and values throughout life. Though a viable personal identity should be operating by the time we are in our twenties, this task needs continuous reworking.

If the ways we celebrate are extensions of our values, then holidays take on a greater meaning. It is not important that the details of holiday practices are perfect, so long as they are meaningful. The stuffing one associates with Thanksgiving, the songs sung at the end of a Passover Seder, or the particular way a family decorates a Christmas tree become etched in our minds. In fact, it is the sameness of these memories that connects past, present, and future.

The second important element in addressing constancy has to do with changing our pace. In order to celebrate, we need to put time and effort into the occasion. The chaos of the Juggler does not make for constancy or satisfaction. Holiday meals need care, the paraphernalia of special days need to be properly stored and retrieved, and most of all, time needs to be set aside. Whether we are acknowledging a birthday or preparing for a religious holiday, there needs to be a careful consideration of what is important.

Modern life is hectic, and it is easy to get caught up in doing everything "on the fly." To create and enact meaningful celebrations, it is crucial to either set aside enough time or consider exercising the choice to postpone or cancel an occasion. Obviously, the best approach is to be deliberate and reasonable in what we expect of ourselves. We do not have to fall into the trap of the Perfectionist. Rather, we have to sort out what is important, and provide the time and plan for implementation. Ironically, if this "work" is done well, each successive holiday becomes easier, for there is no need to continually reinvent the wheel.

Evolutionary Celebration

As much as constancy is at the heart of celebration, so is the process of change. While in some societies and in some cultures, change in celebration is neither expected nor tolerated, that is not the case in the United States. In this part of the world, there is a strong commitment to dynamic growth, sometimes to the point of not leaving well enough alone. Considering that we operate in a context where our ideas, fashions, and technology are in constant flux, we should expect our holidays to be subject to the same dynamics. Change in our celebrations can be initiated by two distinct processes: *natural change* and *necessary change*.

Natural change occurs in both the style of holidays as well as the observance. New technology has created broad interest in the use of outdoor lighting during the winter holidays. In addition to Christian families that use lights in ever more complex patterns, non-Christian families seem to have found colors and patterns which allow them to participate in this end-of-the-year ritual. The result can be so striking that many cities have taken to leaving their holiday lighting in place for much, if not all, of the year.

As a result of the cross-fertilization that comes from being in contact with different families, there is great fascination with incorporating the rituals of other families. This exposure is heightened during the college years, when our children begin to celebrate away from their families of origin, and may take a year or part of a year to study abroad. During this time they have a tremendous exposure to cultural diversity, which they inevitably want to share when they return home. When, for instance, Fran returned from a year abroad in New Zealand, she worked hard to convince her mother to replace the usual baked ham with a leg of lamb for their next Easter dinner, as she had experienced when visiting a host family. After considerable insistence, it would appear that her family has now adopted this dish as their new standard Easter feast.

By the same token, Neal could not come home for Passover one spring, so he was invited to Seder at a college roommate's home in Albuquerque, New Mexico. Unlike his orthodox family, his friend's Passover readings were much more ecumenical, incorporating modern readings on human freedom, which is at the heart of the Passover celebration. Neal, who had been increasingly indifferent toward the holiday, was very impressed. When he was home for the next Passover Seder, he argued strenuously to include readings from Mohandas Gandhi, Martin Luther King, and Thomas Jefferson. While his mother was somewhat open to the idea, his father initially reacted with indignation to modifying the familiar Hagadah. After considerable debate, Neal finally prevailed in convincing his nervous father that including these new readings would allow Neal to feel a new commitment to the holiday. Unfortunately, not all students are so convincing, or all families so accommodating to this natural evolutionary change in holiday ritual.

Even the way in which the myths about Santa Claus have evolved provides evidence for this evolutionary process. Lois relayed a recent heated dialogue that occurred after she began to celebrate Christmas at her own home. Following the death of her father, her house became the center of the Christmas Eve meal. When it came time to prepare the gifts for Christmas morning, her mother was surprised to hear discussion of wrapping the presents that Santa would leave. Her mother said it was improper to wrap Santa's presents, as it would give away the idea that the gifts were given by the parents. Lois and her siblings were annoyed and told her, "This is the way it's done nowadays, Mom." Her mother eventually yielded to this newer tradition, but warned that the wrapping paper should at least be different. Ironically, when her advice on the distinctiveness of the gift wrapping was not heeded, the oldest child was heard commenting to everyone's astonishment, "Hey, Santa uses the same paper as you do, Mom." It would seem that evolution might be best served if newer expressions of tradition pay homage to what is customary.

Sometimes the need to change the framework of celebration is brought about by changes in life circumstances. The most common basis for requiring this mandatory change is marriage or remarriage. Even when marriage takes place between people from similar cultural backgrounds, there will be considerable differences in how celebration is approached. Some people are more religious than others; there are all levels of religious observance, which can change quickly after marriage. Though a couple can claim to be Catholic, for example, they may have very different opinions on how often to attend church services. This same pattern of differences occurs just as frequently with other religious matches.

It is not always the religious holidays that elicit differences. A newly married couple found themselves in a state of conflict with the emphasis her family placed on birthdays. She was accustomed to a lot of attention and gifts, while his family barely acknowledged birthdays. She found herself disappointed and angry after just two years of marriage, as her new husband had a difficult time accepting this change of emphasis. Another couple had strong disagreements about the amount of time they would spend with extended family members. He came from a large family and was used to spending Memorial Day and other secular holidays at gatherings of up to 25 people. She was always bargaining for smaller celebrations, especially when it came to their own birthdays. The occasion that seemed to inevitably exacerbate their differences was New Year's Eve. He wanted to be surrounded by people, while she anticipated an evening of intimacy and solitude. Addressing these differences was difficult, and they had a few years of rocky times until they found a way to compromise.

Perhaps the situation requiring the greatest magnitude of change is the interfaith marriage. Marriage among denominations of Christians has always required accommodation. More recently, the increase in Christian-Jewish marriages has posed a greater problem, especially regarding how to celebrate Christmas. Though couples often proclaim openness to the traditions of their new spouse, things can go awry when they actually have to participate in unfamiliar practices. It is one thing for a Jew to talk about a Christmas tree, but quite another to actually see it in his or her home. The incorporation of another person's heritage can be difficult, even when there is a strong romantic and martial connection.

David and Kay were married less than a year when emotions about Christmas began to run very deep. Based on a few conversations, Kay assumed that David would be eager to assist in getting and decorating their first tree together. David later admitted that he had not given it a great deal of thought. He began to act sullen, but grudgingly went along with Kay's tradition of chopping down a tree and inviting some friends to help decorate it. Though the process was tense, the tree was trimmed, and their apartment was decorated with festive Christmas paraphernalia. The real trouble began when David's Jewish parents announced that they were flying in to spend a few days with the newly weds. They were eager to see their son's new apartment and get to know his wife better. Even though David had grown up in a secular, non-observant household, the thought of his parents confronting a Christmas tree sent him into a panic. He and Kay began to argue about it, and David became insistent that they would have to actually remove the tree from their apartment. Kay could not believe he was serious. She pointed out that his parents did not even celebrate Hanukah, and that David told stories of sitting on Santa's knee in the local department store when he was a child. Emotions ran so high that David actually moved out of their apartment, and the couple separated for three months.

Though the case of David and Kay is extreme, it is repeated with different twists all the time. The differences are not always religious. Sometimes they are ethnic, sometimes social, and increasingly, they are racial. David and Kay eventually got back together by starting marital psychotherapy. They learned that their rift could have been avoided if they had recognized that their heritages would pose problems with celebrations. If they had embarked on the difficult task of respectful negotiation, they would have been able to manage the deep feelings that almost ruined their marriage. If extended family is the key to resolving perceived differences, they might have to become involved. In David's case, with therapeutic guidance he was surprised to find that his parents were less reactive than he expected. Once they had accepted the intermarriage, they expected that there would be an accommodation of Kay's traditions. All realized that ongoing discussion was necessary, especially concerning issues of child rearing. David and Kay found, however, that if they were willing to engage in a constructive, honest dialogue, the problems would not be insurmountable.

Unfortunately, people do not always behave in a reasonable way. Even with professional intervention, some families cannot accept deviation from their own traditions. Often, they can be quite inconsistent. On the one hand, they embrace the "outsider" and accept him/her into their family. However, when it comes time for First Holy Communion, a bar mitzvah, or a wedding, sometimes it boils down to who will conduct the ceremony. For celebration to occur in a way that is meaningful to all, respect has to be given to both of the couple's traditions. It is unfortunate when compromise does not work. In such cases, it may be necessary to declare loyalties and risk alienation within a family. This often occurs in the offspring of immigrant parents, who simply have a dreadful time with the concept of assimilation. If a new marriage is going to stand the crossfire from disgruntled in-laws, limits may have to be set. *Commitment must be to the spouse!* In a majority of instances, the displeased parents, given time, will come around and feel less threatened by the novelty of the holiday.

Vacation:
The Unstructured Holiday

Though most holidays occur over a day or a long weekend, vacations can range from days to weeks to a month if one is fortunate. Moreover, in other parts of the world, people refer to vacations as "holidays," and tend to treat them with the same reverence. Vacations do, in fact, evoke blues patterns similar to those of other holidays. Some people find it very difficult to take vacations, because breaking away from their ordinary routines raises considerable anxiety. Others find the task of vacation planning to be quite onerous, as they are uncertain about what will meet their needs. Couples and families can also find that the sustained nature of a vacation can actually expose conflict that may be masked by everyday life.

There are two main types of vacations: first, a rest/refresher experience and, second, a change or stimulating getaway. This is an important distinction, since it is not always clear which is more desirable, and to whom. The problem is further compounded by the lack of ample vacation time in our crowded work lives. There is no question that most Americans do not take enough personal holiday time. Unlike our European counterparts, we must cram vacation into a week or two per year. This capacity to sustain an unbalanced work life seems to cut across all socio-economic groups. Many work situations allow only two weeks, while top-level professionals are often unskilled in breaking away from their self-determined, multi-layered work schedules.

The rest vacation is not as straightforward as it sounds. Unlike other prescribed holidays, this one calls for a person to determine what is actually restful. It is important to try to minimize the presence of stress in this type of experience. Sufficient time needs to be set aside to get to and from the location where one will rest. Too often, the goal is an exotic, faraway island where the process involves plane changes and complex land connections. Unless the vacation is for at least a week, the strain of such travel contradicts the notion of a restful experience. Power vacations or quick getaways have a chic appeal but are, undoubtedly, not restful.

There is something to be said for developing and maintaining a degree of ritual in restful vacations. If you find a place that is compatible with your needs, strong consideration should be given to making it an annual ritual. Going back to the same beach house, country cottage, or resort can be very comforting. You needn't use energy exploring the terrain, identifying local resources, or trying to meet new people. Some vacations are associated with novelty, but not this one. It is far better to be able to anticipate the sights and sounds of familiar terrain. Even if it is only for a week or two per year, it is quite possible to develop seasonal acquaintances which, over the years, can develop into deep friendships.

Moving from a fast-paced busy schedule to unstructured time is not always easy. People of all ages commonly report that they feel bored because "there is nothing to do." It is easy to forget that the task of rest is to shift into a mode of low stimulation. Unfortunately, too many of us do not allow ourselves to go through a period of "decompression." Like children, we can become agitated and begin to fill our time with activities and schedules. We go on vacation to break with our regimented lives, only to find that we have imposed nonessential time demands. The more plans we make on this type of vacation, the faster time appears to move. When we leave our schedule open and become involved in such activities as reading, fishing, hiking, or simply watching the clouds drift by, we seem to gain a sense of increased time.

A big issue for many people is how much they are able to disconnect from their work life. While it is easy to suggest disconnecting from the demands of the job, this is sometimes impossible. Many of us have careers in which we go off on holiday while things are pending. When this is the case, it might be better to maintain contact rather than be in the dark about unresolved matters. A shop owner claimed that he would feel more relaxed on vacation if he simply called his store twice daily rather than feel tied up waiting for the telephone to ring. This is in contrast to a financial planner who brings his laptop along and, to the dismay of his wife, maintains contact with his office on a steady and distracting basis. When it comes to modern technological tools such as fax machines and portable computers, the rule is simple: Leave them at home.

One idea that goes against the grain is that we might take a holiday by simply staying at home. Most people will occasionally call in sick and take off a day or a long weekend. However, travel and expense can be avoided by disconnecting from work life, and perhaps letting associates think you are away while you enjoy the comforts of your home. Most busy people are afraid that they will succumb to their normal routines. However, with a reasonable amount of personal discipline, it is possible to enjoy the environment most people work so hard to create. Digging into hobbies or completing minor home-based projects for which we never seem to have time can be truly renewing. Those fortunate enough to have a pleasant place to sit outdoors can accomplish essential reading or correspondence without using precious time waiting for delayed planes, or sitting in gridlocked beach traffic.

Vacations not only give us the chance to recover our energy; they also provide the opportunity to extend ourselves. Early in life, the plea begins, "What are we going to do today?" This desire for stimulation starts in childhood and continues into older age. In fact, when most people are interviewed about retirement, they inevitably include travel in their scheme. Obviously, the need for novelty in our lives is directly related to the amount of free time available. Abraham Maslow, the humanistic psychologist, pointed out the desire to grow or actualize ourselves occurs when more fundamental needs are met. Thus, in developing countries where the work cycle does not easily permit leisure time, there is not the same premium on self-enhancement; life itself is enough of an adventure.

The question of how to enhance ourselves or our children is not always without challenge. As we have seen, the structured holidays can trigger anxiety, depression, and anger for many reasons which have been developed. An adventure or activity-based vacation has the same evocative potential. The Lost Soul, for example, does not know what to do or with whom to do it. The Juggler makes plans which are probably too complex or too expensive, and ends up anxious or unsatisfied because the experience is anything but a vacation. The Perfectionist drives himself and others crazy by planning, analyzing, and over-controlling every aspect of the trip. We have probably all been in the company of a traveling Perfectionist who has an ironclad plan for every minute of every day and can tolerate no deviation.

Adventure vacations are by definition not supposed to be stress-free. If we are to grow, there has to be new learning and the overcoming of obstacles. When we sign on for a physical, Outward Bound type of experience, we are asking to be challenged. By the same token, when we commit to traveling in another country, we will be pressured by differences in food and language, as well with the strains associated with time changes and luggage movement. Though the goal of such holidays is obviously not to produce stress, the value we derive seems to be related to how we are "stretched." A teenage inner-city boy, who had been given a scholarship to an Outward Bound sailing trip on the Chesapeake, summed up this point when he said, "I was never so scared in my life, but dealing with that storm has changed me forever."

Since there are no rules or guidelines for what kind of trip you should take, it is always worthwhile to reflect, first, on how a particular venture meets your needs. There is a time when traveling to foreign lands will be energizing and stimulating. At other points in life, the acquisition of a new skill such as fly-fishing or taking an intensive course in a favorite sport such as tennis or golf could be perfect. Too often, being unsure about what makes the most sense, people will opt for what is easy and available. While these "packaged" experiences can be satisfying, it seems much more rewarding to be the architect of your own adventures. Though figuring out vacation plans is harder, it is more consistent with the message of this book: *Let celebration be an expression of our own values as much as possible.*

Vacations, like all holidays, provide opportunities to deepen significant relationships. The combination of adults' work schedules, children's school schedules, and other obligations makes family getaways especially difficult. Finding a workable time slot often takes energetic planning, especially as children begin to have schedules of their own. Apart from the ritual of visiting a Disney resort, it is often unclear how to satisfy the family as a whole. Sometimes the planning process can be so tedious that the family vacation never quite happens.

Everyone with small children should probably watch a video of *National Lampoon's Vacation,* in which Chevy Chase stars as the indomitable, boneheaded father who drags his family of four across the country to get to a California theme park (which is closed when they arrive). En route, the family encounters a series of comic misadventures which are instigated by the dad's insistence on exposing them toa cliched itinerary of the "American Experience". This scenario, though not always comic, is played out all the time as families struggle to find what will be meaningful to all members. The main principle to be followed on this subject is simple: You must be completely mindful of the ages and interests of family members. As with most other holiday problems, solutions reside with open communication and respect. Though children are not always the best judge of what will be interesting, they need to be heard. Probably no one should to be subjected to one of those interminable car trips where dad is intent on meeting predetermined schedules with little or no time for those dreaded "pit stops."

The Transmission of Holidays

When we are young, before we leave our own families, holidays are experienced in a less pressured way. It is fascinating to watch the transformation that usually takes place when new parents face the task of creating celebrations for a child. Before having a family, many college students and young adults can be somewhat casual about the significance of special days. There might even be mild disdain for all the fuss that goes into these holiday productions. In any event, many young people are content to participate without feeling responsible for making the day special.

This role as observer changes dramatically as soon as they feel the responsibility that comes with parenting. A great sense of urgency appears when new parents realize that they are suddenly responsible for first communions, bar mitzvahs, and even the loss of that first baby tooth. Do they perpetuate myths about the tooth fairy and, if so, how much money should be left under the pillow? Another question which quickly arises has to do with which holidays will be acknowledged, and how. Most new parents are somewhat caught off guard, and have an initial tendency to replicate the experiences that were so dear to them.

The desire to bathe children in ritual, sentimentality, and faith is the nucleus of what holidays are all about in the first place. Santa Claus, the tooth fairy, the Easter bunny, and other figures associated with holidays provide a mechanism for maintaining the innocence of childhood. The realities and exigencies of life become harsh all too soon as children must learn to deal with cruelty, sickness, and other aspects of life which simply seem unfair. *Holidays become a vehicle through which magic can prevail, to help us all transcend ordinary life.* Most children are quite reluctant to give up their belief in a Santa Claus, and most parents work hard to help maintain that belief.

As we have moved toward a more secular, naturalistic way of life, our capacity to dream and hope has been compromised. Our myths and symbols are more difficult to convey without the support of religious systems which provide the foundation for belief in structures that cannot be rationally defined. Not too long ago, children's imaginations were stirred by Grimm's fairy tales and classic nursery rhymes. The rise of television, the VCR, and the computer seem to have reduced the role of this classic oral and written literature in the development of children. Nevertheless, we still see the tremendous power of fantasy in the lives of children, as they seem to adore the animated films based on such classic tales.

Children have not changed as much as our capacity to nourish their imagination. Christian children continue to be fascinated by the Christmas story, just as young Jewish children relish the retelling of the story of Passover at each Seder. Children still love to be read to, alone or in groups. They still crave letting their fantasies and imaginations run wild as they listen to frightening stories of giants, dragons, ghosts, and even of wolves that devour her grandmother when a little girl is clearly disobedient.

The urgency we feel when it is time to provide holiday magic is rooted in a lack of confidence about how to enact celebration. It is always interesting to speak to older folks about this question of holiday know-how. Our parents, and especially our grandparents, really knew how to prepare and conduct a celebration. They seemed to possess ample time and competence to prepare the holiday feast, and to lead a ritual without confusion or uncertainty. In contemporary society, there is a great deal of insecurity about playing the role of holiday magician. The best explanation centers on a failure in transmission from one generation to another. It is amazing to hear people say, "I've seen the Hanukah candles lit so many times, but I actually don't know how to do it myself."

The two elements essential to the successful transmission of holiday competence are clarity of purpose and participation in preparation. The point has been made over and over that holiday celebrations need to be connected to their core meaning. Children are always fascinated by the religious beliefs or folklore concerning holidays. So many modern parents ignore the opportunity to spend some time clarifying why a special day is celebrated. Even as we have become more secularized, it is still possible to explain the personal meaning of a holiday. Children love to hear stories about their parents' childhoods, and holidays are a perfect time to convey a picture of themselves and their beliefs.

Nothing turns children off more than glaring hypocrisy, which can become all too apparent during holidays. Especially during holidays that are clearly religious in nature, the celebrations should not take on a zealousness which is inconsistent with a family's usual manner of observance. Clergy from every religious denomination are painfully aware of those members of their congregations who "put on a show" for major holidays. Children, too, eventually experience the same disdain, which can translate into indifference when their parents are not reasonably committed to the practices they are preaching. Unless there is a clear observance, communicated through everyday practice, it is very meaningful to pause and explain what rituals are all about. Probably one of the main reasons that so many modern parents fall short on this task is that it was not done for them, and they simply do not have an explanation at hand.

Every elementary school teacher knows that participation is the key to learning. Children acquire skills when they have the opportunity to be interactive with the tools they are learning to use. It would be folly, for example, to teach writing or computer literacy without an opportunity to actually perform the relevant functions. By the same token, we can eat Thanksgiving stuffing over and over without any sense of how it is prepared. It is not uncommon for children with gifted parents to not be the beneficiary of those skills. A great carpenter's child will feel uncomfortable working with wood, unless the child has actually built something himself. Though some learning can take place through simple observation and imitation, the desire is not the same as when there is participation,

It takes time and patience to generate the right kind of interactive climate. Jugglers, for example, can never include anyone or delegate very well because of the pace they maintain. If children are to be included in holiday preparations, everything must slow down to their pace. If the pace is too rapid, children begin to feel incompetent and lose interest. It is obvious that Perfectionists, too, cannot do a very good job of allowing children to participate in the staging of holidays. In their case, too much emphasis on getting things right leaves little room for the errors which are an inevitable and essential part of the learning process.

It is paradoxical when parents feel they are doing holidays for their children, but somehow lose their interest in the process. There is tremendous satisfaction when the mission of conveying the values and skills associated with celebration is successful. Children are given the protection afforded by myth, belief, and fantasy, while parents are able to stir their imaginations, and affirm what is important.

Celebration As a Mirror

As we anticipate the next holiday, we tend to think of those for whom we truly care. We look forward to seeing them—even when the gatherings are not always fully positive. This annual amnesia is not all bad, as each celebration provides us an opportunity to seek and give affirmation to our loved ones. Part of being "present" is seizing the opportunity to maximize the time we spend, especially when contemporary patterns of mobility have our families in different and distant regions. We should take the time to listen, and acknowledge what everyone is doing. *We should use the holidays as a chance to strengthen our connections, simply by paying attention to what is important in each other's lives.* This process of attentiveness provides us with a picture of ourselves, and the people to whom we are connected.

We go back to our families of origin, where we can immerse ourselves in our past as well as our present. It is sometimes a relief to be seen not in terms of your achievements, but by your status as parent, child, uncle, or grandmother. These designations are powerful in both a positive and negative sense. When family relations are working well, we feel appreciated and accepted, independently of what else we have been doing. The movie star goes home and is treated just like everyone else; she can relax and not have to worry about living up to her image. By the same token, someone who has had personal disappointment or failure can join significant relatives and feel the healing power of acceptance. When acceptance and appreciation are consistently absent from holidays, I strongly recommend the exercising of choice. Families can exercise their power in all kinds of ways, and it is critical that we understand the effect of being in the company of those whom we expect to care about us.

One of the reasons we look in a mirror is to take stock of our appearance and consider adjustments. We can simply fix our hair, adjust our tie, or, when things really look bad, consider changing our outfit. The same can be said of our holidays, what they mean, and with whom we choose to celebrate. Though the roles of constancy and routine are central to celebration, it is crucial to remember that we do not have to tolerate sustained negative experience when we are expecting celebration and affirmation.

Tyrone was a 38-year-old African-American who was struggling in his work as a shipping executive. He began therapy to explore whether he should resume his education and try to complete two more years of law school. He had always wanted to be a judge, but dropped out of law school in order to support his wife and two young children. Though his wife was ready to return to work as an elementary school teacher, Tyrone was not sure he still had the drive to pursue a legal career. Shortly after he began therapy he became very angry and distracted as his 39th birthday approached. He explained that he hated the way his parents responded to his birthday, and found himself upset every year.

Tyrone claimed that his annual birthday celebration

stirred up everything that was wrong with his relationship with his parents. Things had never been the same since he lost his younger brother in a car accident, when Tyrone was 20. Though his brother, Neil, had always "seemed" to be the favorite, after his death Tyrone perceived that his relationship with his parents really deteriorated. He would receive a token phone call on his birthday, with the question, "What can we get you?" He resented the question and would usually reply that they really did not need to get him anything. It turned out that his parents usually did not buy him a present. This particular year they offered to take him and his family out to dinner, but said it would have to be on a different day because of his mother's church function. Tyrone did not express much emotion, but became furious as the time for the dinner approached.

With his wife's support, Tyrone decided that his birthday was a symptom of some deeper problem with his parents. He decided to rock the boat. Rather than go through another painful experience, he telephoned them and asked for a separate meeting with no other family members present. After overcoming significant resistance from both parents, he persuaded his father that they had to meet. The process actually took place on three occasions, and involved some powerful emotional exchanges. Finally, Tyrone learned something that really put him into a tailspin. His parents had never told him that he had been adopted, and that two years later they had biologically conceived his brother. They had planned to tell him when he turned 21, but could never face the subject after Neil's untimely death.

This birthday confrontation actually opened up some critical deficiencies in Tyrone's family. His mother eventually admitted that she had distanced herself from him after losing her younger child. She was aware of some conflicts concerning which son had been lost, and was determined to never let Tyrone feel that he was less loved than his deceased brother. As so often happens when deep feelings are avoided, the feared prophecy becomes fulfilled. Tyrone, indeed, felt less loved by his parents even though they were trying to "protect" him.

Tyrone's initial reactions were sadness, rage, and disgust. He vowed to sever ties with his parents for withholding such important information. After a few months passed, and he decided not to search for his biological parents, Tyrone agreed to begin family therapy with his adoptive parents. Though the process is not complete, it has been inspirational on two fronts. First, it demonstrates the powerful healing inherent in open communication and the damage which avoidance can cause. Second and most germane to the central thesis of this book is that a holiday offered a format for assessment and change. The negative emotions associated with his birthday were a reflection of bigger issues in Tyrone's family history. After some careful self-examination, Tyrone had the courage to stop the toxic process.

For the most part, blues patterns are not caused by the traditions we hold dear. On the contrary, too many of our universal and personal holidays have been compromised and diluted by unresolved conflict and self-defeating approaches to celebration. There is usually no need for the reinvention of our rituals. When we have adequately reflected on the dynamics of our holiday malaise, adjustments can be made, either to ourselves or the manner in which we celebrate.

Recalling that ritual and constancy are at the heart of celebration, we must still exercise a pro-active creativity. When a theater director is charged with the staging of a

Shakespeare play, there is ample room to exercise latitude while staying true to the essence of the art. Celebration provides us with the opportunity to underscore what we hold sacred through the process of meaningful reenactment. In being both a member of the audience and a potential director, each of us has the capacity to shape and control the vibrancy of our celebrations and our lives.

Happy Holidays!

Index